Chakras & Healing For Beginners

Your Self-Love, Care & Awakening
Journey- Guided Mindfulness
Meditations, Crystals, Kundalini,
Empath & Psychic Abilities, Reiki,
Yoga & More

Outline

Introduction

Welcome to an exciting new chapter in your life! You are finally going to get answers for the ways you've been feeling lately and why they are related to larger themes. This book will help you create a language around spiritual awakening. An experience you find yourself currently in the middle of. It was no coincidence you would choose this book to read– it means you are on the path, listening to your intuitive abilities, and are safely guided.

There is a lot of information out there about what healing your Chakras looks like and how to heal yourself energetically, but in a separate sort of way. Only taking into account each even as it happens instead of looking at the whole picture. This book invites you to take a harder look at what's possible for healing. In the end, this text is meant to separate all of your specific experiences, help you see the importance of each and every encounter, and then show you how they heal you as a whole. You are given full permission to synthesize the events in life to create one large theme and when this is done, we create hope. When you leave your heart and mind open to seeing all of the synchronicities, you reach the next stages of conscious evolution.

For the sake of taking this information in, you are encouraged to look at each of the subjects we mention as ways of being awake and aware of your existence– how many of them show up for you?

Utilizing the 50+ guided meditations provided at the end of this book will help solidify what you've learned and create slow steps toward moving forward in a positive, new light. Feel free to connect to whatever meditation feels right for you and when. Another way to direct your energy is to do a meditation after each section if you have the time and are in a safe place to do so. None of the meditations should be done in the car or in a place where your attention is a matter of life or death. However most of them can be practiced in public spaces or in the car while waiting for an event.

Its important to remember that healing your Chakras, increasing your energy, and waking up to the purpose of your life are slow and gradual steps towards success. Sometimes it may take us years to understand the fullness of what is happening to us, all we need to remember is that nothing needs to happen over night.

This book is to offer you a vast array of knowledge about the sensitive inner workings of your being, take care to be in safe places while taking in this important information, the frequency and absorption will have larger and positive affect.

You will gain ancient connected intelligence to who you are and the energy and frequency that your body is made up of. This is a step-by-step approach to Awakening the Kundalini through developing simple, yet effective practices to open the Third Eye and dive deeper into the depths of who you are.

It is recommended that you consider some important factors before moving forward, as this journey is one that blossoms with each passing day. The subtleties culimate to the larger picture of change, its truly being awake to the greater purpose of your presence in this magnifcent time in our rapid changing history.

Are you ready to embark on a fun and challenging adventure to another side of yourself?
Some parts of you will be re-awakened, childlike intentions, memories good/bad, dreams and aspirations of the past may resurface.

Are you be willing to shift and move to accommodate your life with new habits?
Having a private space where you can naturally work on your new process is very important—even a closet will do. Consider if you are available to make small changes necessary to get where you want to be.

Are you prepared to have the way you are perceived by others to change?
Many people will have comments about who you are after some months of working with your bodies

energy system and they many not all be as positive as you hope. Questions may arise that make you feel uncomfortable because you will be noticed in ways you weren't before.

Are you ready for the time of your life?
When you are awakened again from a long slumber you start to notice the small synchronistic events as they pop up in your awareness more each day. Following the practices outlined in this book will guide you to practices that give gratitude to these "coincidences" --we more correctly define as synchronicity– and make you even more aware to gauge the best routes to take, the best foods to eat, and when to reach for a positive connection with another person.

Are you ready to emotionally level up?
Emotional maturity increases with this work as you work through your own emotional process and your part in relationships whether it be work, romantic, friendship or familial–the dynamic will start to shift. You will feel more inclined to take responsibility regardless if you are right or wrong and that's true freedom at heart. This will open you up for genuine interactions, deeper love connections and understanding with people you want in your life.

Are you ready to redefine your relationships?
When you listen to the inner callings of healthy and safe relationships you understand where your participation begins and where other's participation

ends. The approach is to get comfortable clarifying what you hope to establish with these relationships and together devise a way to refine the way you approach one another. When we create a safe space, when we come with a responsible nature and even disposition, we connect deeply to the people we come in contact with. Reception is a likely reaction as you approach the situation with hopes of reach a healthy conclusion– it can be seen as an act of healing and moving forward.

Do you desire to rewire you mental tapes?
Has anyone ever told you that you are not the voice inside your head? As you navigate through the pages of this book, you will start to see how often you speak to yourself, you will start to identify its effect on your body and learn how to redirect that speech towards greater love and appreciation for yourself and those you surround yourself with.

Chapter One:
New Perspectives on Spiritual Awakening

Spiritual awakening looks like a lot of different things for many people and no experience or journey is exactly the same. The names, faces, and chain of events will all differ on some level. It can be comforting to know when someone has a similar experience as yours and it can also feel good to know that your experience resinates on deep levels across the universe. We are all here with some level of healing or awareness to stumble upon. However its very important that you don't identify with anyone else's story but your own.

Some people get rapped up in that good feeling of being connected and feel a certain affinity towards make their experience meld with other's. Almost like a collective experience of pain and triumph. While that may be true in retrospect, getting lost in another account of what really happened to you can lead to undue hurt and disappointment at a later date. All too often people are leaving behind a life of freedom by understanding their spiritual experience to instead go back to religion because they felt "duped" or led to believe something that wasn't true.

It is stressed that you write down all of your accounts of your personal experience by Journaling and recording video is a great option too. Having the chance to go back on what you went through can not only be cathartic, but telling about the cycles and ways you circle around the same subjects. Taking notice is important for these reasons.

This chapter will explore the many ways we can wake up to see our lives in a new light. These are gentle descriptions of what it looks like when you are looking within. You can experience one or all of the many rights of passage below.

A misconception with Spiritual Awakening is that everything becomes rosy in our lives, we no longer experience pain, we are master mediators and removed from conflict. This is not what Awakening brings even though these experiences occur much more often and for longer periods of time.

What is to be obtained is a sense of what it feels like to physically and mentally understand the concept of how to Awaken parts of yourself. To know what part of the body it is when someone mentions that their Solar Plexus seems blocked and to know the remedy to loosen the knots and get back to a state of equilibrium.

Spiritual Awakening is being equipped to deal with parts of life that seem difficult and hard to surpass. It's having a toolbox full of remedies that soothe, heal, and give strength to your inner being. It is a close connection to the subtle parts of life that stack on top of each other–making life feel beautiful in all of its quirky imperfections.

Below are a few things you may notice more right out the gate and you are encouraged to milk them for as long as you can–make the moment last.

-Birds singing, insects moving, and lustrous cloud formations in the sky. You are encouraged to look up anytime you have the chance to be outside.

-Interactions with people are so pleasant– the sweeter you are, the better the conversation. You leave better than when you arrived.

-Things you have been desiring start to show themselves again and opportunities to obtain them are closer within reach.

-You start to see your thoughts in books you read, podcast's you listen to, and conversations you overhear.

-People reaching out to you that have been on your mind or vice versa.

-Patience creeps upon you, realizing that the longer you wait, the more financially accessible it becomes.

-Overall pride of who you are and where you have come from.

-Encounters with certain people become noticeable– do they feed your spirit or bring you to a place you didn't want to be?

What to remember is there is no end goal to this process, it's a lifelong journey from here on out, and your experience will look different than those you see on Youtube or read on Blog posts. You are greatly encouraged to not compare yourself to others as it only complicates the situation and assigns feelings that don't serve your newly developed self.

Perfection or the right "look" should not be the focus because the more imperfect we are at something gives us the gift of true experience– its not a contest on who does it best. If you see behaviors or read about others that exude this, stay far away, it will not serve you.

The intention of this book is to connect you to knowledge that sits dormant inside your bodies design and as you open up you'll realize you have much more inside that needs self expression– stumbling on talents and hobbies you have long forgotten or didn't even know was a passion come back once again. In no way is this book to serve over your internal guidance system and intuition, nor take the place of your prescribed therapies. Please listen to yourself and only begin another section when you feel comfortable with where you are.

Life-Changing Events

Events in our lives can begin to reach a climax as realizations start to come into view. You will notice certain situations come up more frequently, luck, as you would have it has seemed to vanish. Events that change our lives sometimes go unnoticed. Have you ever stepped into a new life you were unaware you were living? What if someone close to you exclaimed, "man ,you've changed"! Would you feel perplexed by the statement or are you aware of the events in your life that shape your decisions and peoples perceptions of you? If it's the latter, congratulations! If you find yourself in the first scenario, never fear! We all start from this place of not knowing who we are and waking up to remember again. Sometimes its due to looking within that you find the meanings and a lot of times it takes someone to say something out loud that brings your change to the forefront of your mind.

While life changing events in fact do change us, we have to remember at a core level where we have come from and where we hope to land. Utilizing the events that happen in your life as a nudge toward better and bigger meaning offers compassion to your situation. This is the time to start looking at these events as positive reinforcement of what's good for you and what isn't, what needs to be let go of and what doesn't. This train of thought will not work for tragic, unforseen accidents, these events are not within reach to understand and take on to ourselves, nor is it fair. What's good for you and not is taking stalk of how your life feels after these events.

Asking these questions can help you sort out how you feel about some events that have changed your life lately. Nothing is black or white, but looking at your perception in an objective point of view can give more insight than just assuming you feel some kind of way.

$Do I feel good about where my life is?
$Are there things that happened to me that need healing?
$Do I feel strong or weak from my recent experiences?
$Does it feel like I've restarted my life?
$Do I see myself fully?
$Can I accept what's happened and move on?
$Can you I this in a positive light?

Soul Mates

The role of Soul mate takes on a larger meaning then what you may have previously considered. Soul mates are Soul's that are connected to one another through a long and deep energetic connection. It can be often described as a rush of blood to the cheeks, a quickened heartbeat or longing feelings about a person you don't know. When people think of this term it is usually seen as the person you understand and are understood by the most. What people don't fully grasp is a lot of times a Soul mate isn't necessarily here to make you happy, to provide your wildest dreams or read your mind. Soul mates show up to progress us forward, no matter what the end result of the relationship is.

Soul mates can be your mother, father, aunt, uncle, cousin, best friend, lover, man at the corner store, and your childhood crush. It could be anyone that hears you and acts in such a way that you end up making better choices, moving on from pain, or taking a leap of faith. Sometimes they are the really bad boyfriend/girlfriend or parent who verbally abuses you so you get the courage to finally stand up for yourself when its truly needed. Its also noticing when people overstep your boundaries because its happened so many times. Sometimes they are your dad, showing up whenever you needed him and feeling as if your points of view have been understood. It can also manifest your 10th grade history teacher that pushed you to write a report about a subject that changed your life, interests, and focus. What you'll notice is these people stepped in to guide you to the safest and most successful place based on how they "know you"– Soul mates have a special way of knowing exactly how to show up for you.

Looking back on all the people you have encountered over the years, how many of them felt intense, familiar, and magnetic? Does their voice sound familiar, or do they repeat things from trusted people that have passed on? Do they look like someone you remember from your past? Its wise to dissect the relationships you hold dear to your heart. It can be healing to venture into why they feel so good in your life and to consider if you feel you've been connected for far longer than this current lifetime. Opening your mind to this expanse offers yet another opportunity for compassion. You will fine tune your empathy towards people that light you up and those that push every button in the book to help you leave.

Soul mates are no longer the notion about the one person you connect with on a Soul level, in fact, there are many Souls that you will connect with in this life. This experience can be had easier if you're able to open yourself up to the possibility of having more than one. Sink into the vast array of relationships you can have while being connected to your many Soul mates.

Understanding Soul mates, what they do for us, and how they show up in our lives to push us forward gives healing to the energetic centers of the body and keeps the Chakra system fluid– ready to take on life. Soul mates will be placed strategically whilst on your journey to remind you that you are not alone. There is always someone to guide the path whether they actually live in the ways you do, they understand the larger meaning of your life, or strive, sometimes unconsciously, to help you get their. Taking some time to reflect on these people in your life, naming them, and keeping contact (if possible) are great ways to keep yourself open to new Souls that may need to enter and effect change in you.

The Role Of Dreams

Dreams play a big role in how we perceive our reality. Subconsciously we live in a different world when we close our eyes, playing out scenarios we may never get to experience in the waking state. Dreams will play an important factor in helping you wake up to the healing that needs to take place. You may start to have more vivid dreams that visit you during different parts of your waking state and all throughout the day, solidifying the themes you felt while sleeping.

Writing your dreams down can outline the common language that occurs. This may help you tie together one large theme out of 10 days of observation and feeling your way through the memory. Some people experience the dream state as another world they get to function in and be the main character of. Tackling major obstacles, building things with a group of people, or having a visit from your ex can take on a much more important meaning. To take this further, is there any dream you remember that is far off into the past? Can you remember more than one specific dream in your life that either repeats itself while you sleep or does it repeats itself in your mind during the waking state? When you evaluate these, is there a common person, animal, feeling or suggestion you get? Its important to write them down as the act of turning an ethereal thought into the physical form of writing may give reasoning or depth.

Another consideration about the dream state and its importance to spiritual awakening and healing is becoming fine tuned in listening while watching the subconscious mind at work. Learning more about dream interpretations and meanings may open more memory and unlock more story telling. Discussing your feelings and findings with a trusted friend may invite a new perspective into your experience.

If you are a person who does not dream, or can't remember them, you are encouraged to repeat this affirmation before you go to bed to suggest to your mind and body that you're ready for the messages that lay dormant in your subconscious mind. Please write the affirmation down on a small piece of paper and put it under your pillow. Leave the piece of affirmation paper under your pillow and repeat the affirmation below nightly.

"May I remember my dreams tonight as I fall asleep easily and quickly. I give my mind permission to catalogue what it see's and report it back to me after I wake. May I be safe on my journey to the unknown and return unharmed. And so it is."

We offer a few tips to continue the even flow of your dream state:

$Keep a healthy sleeping space by washing your bedding weekly.
$Clean out all the corners of your sleeping area, leaving nothing untouched or out of its place.

$Cleansing your room with candles or incense while opening the windows offers release for new things to come in.

Synchronicity

Events in our lives start to take a larger meaning when we observe. Taking a longer look at what happens to us day to day and moment by moment starts to formulate our reality. It is said that when you are on a spiritual journey to awakening you start to honestly be awake to your life. Awareness around how you feel and subjective meanings are the road to seeing the light within yourself.

Synchronicity is seeing an event and attaching it to something bigger, orchestrated, and outside of yourself to prove there is more to life than the mundane. For example, you arrive late to your flight no matter how may fail safes you put in the night before. You woke up late even though your alarm when off because you pressed snooze too many times. It took longer than usual for the water to heat up in your apartment for a shower, giving you major anxiety every time you looked at the clock. Because of this, you decide to schedule your pickup by Uber early so you can at least be ahead of something. But wait, where is the app? You frantically go to the app store to purchase Uber, enter your information and get a ride to your place. You were supposed to have been at the airport an hour ago because you know security check out will be crazy. In the end, you hear your flight being called as you remove your shoes, belt, and laptop into the x-ray machine...reschedule time. You go to the counter to reschedule your flight and to your surprise, they are going to let you sit in the last first class seat on a flight leaving in 1 hour and will take less time than the first flight you booked. Dang. How did that happen? Synchronicity.

Now think back to how many events over your life that have occurred in some way as explained above. What happens to you even though you plan against it and how many times have you laughed to yourself thinking... "that was better than my initial plan"? Can you think of anything that was a long list of events that got you to being a parent, successful business person, or great student? Notice what has been done to you or around you might have been for you after all. What positive conclusions can we come to when looking for synchronicity?

Sensing A Shift

What does sensing a shift really mean? Sure we all notice from time to time when something changes or feels slightly different, but what does it mean to sense a radical shift? A shift can represent anything different than what we are used to in terms of time, routines, and people. It can also represent the feeling of knowing things can never go back to the way they used to, or knowing some impending consequence will come.

Why does sensing shift matter when healing the Chara's or energy? Why would shifts make any difference to you when going through a spiritual awakening? When you FEEL the difference without having to see it, you have developed a perception past what others can identify for you. The awareness around what it takes to sense something different than the supposed current reality is a sense perception that shouldn't be taken lightly. It's the sure fire way to determine if what you are doing is actually providing you any benefit. If things stay the same, you do not grow

A shift in time feels a lot like being outside of yourself, seeing that things are the same, but noticing that they feel different inside of your body. Time going really fast or markedly slow can be another way we interpret a time shift. A shift in routine feels like a drastic change towards something new that is propelled by new meaning and beliefs, one's that you had no inclination of the day before, such as waking up and realizing you're done smoking cigarettes.

Spiritual Teachers

The role of spiritual teachers has always remained a pertainment factor in a persons evolution to a better life. There are concepts and ideas one may not be able to read in a book or experience on their own. The element of being able to bounce your ideas off of someone else and receive constructive criticism is sometimes extremely important for certain people– not all. Spiritual teachers offer a direct connection to particular lineages and can hold the keys to what makes a successful life.

However the role of spiritual teachers has lost its context, not over the years, but in a general sense. When power of thought, ideation, and practice is left to another person to decide, the encounters for abuse increase– a natural human reaction to power. That's why it is wise to do your research and to seek a person who helps lead you to your own realizations, not someone who dictates to you what those realizations are.

Finding a spiritual teacher may be a bit of a battle because they don't exactly tout their services out in the open, if they do, take caution. This person will be the yogi who opened the studio up the street and has a devout spiritual practice. They may be an intuitive who over the years, has developed systems and practices that have worked for their own lives. If this person follows something outside of themselves combined with real world evidence of change and growth, they could be a spiritual teacher. See, they don't exactly need to be a person that is declared a spiritual teacher, but rather a person who has spiritual principles you'd like to learn from.

"Spiritual teacher" red flags:
$A spiritual teacher is not doing the things they suggest to the people they give advice to.
$They are not consistent in their behavior or emotions and feel untrustworthy.
$They ask you for money without providing any real spiritual service.
$You find they are caught up in lies or defamatory

claims.

$They participate in unhealthy practices that dim their light.

$They are negative or invoke constant states of anger as a way of understanding.

$They hurt others or are derogatory to people unnecessarily.

$Do not display compassion for all diverse creatures.

$Do not respect or consider the earth and its resources.

$Inappropriate or unwanted behavior.

$Taking advantage of other's or their emotional vulnerability.

The Awakening Journey

The awakening journey is one of pain, understanding and triumph. When you have awakened to your life you start to realize all of the fallacies that held you back from following your true feelings or desires. What comes to be is a story about why your life has come to this tipping point of change, breaking through what doesn't fit your natural, intended storyline. Again, the journey of awakening spiritually will look different from person to person, but in actuality, the spark is always built around the breakthrough of truth.

Truth is what an awakening journey is intended to draw out of you and the process in which it occurs can be colorful and a bit cruel, it the end, the universe hopes you are able to laugh about it. The way we arrive to truth is what looks different for us all, the pain and hurt around what keeps us small can vary from a small instance to a whole lifetime of disappointment and lack of connection. In the end, no matter how long or in which way's we were hurt, we follow the same path and the emotions that erupt within us feel the same regardless of the circumstance.

The awakening journey does not always get recorded or accounted for because people don't actually know when or how its happening. There is no manual explaining all the different subtleties that can occur and sum up what a spiritual journey would look like, until now. You may not get that lovely shock and awe into beauty and understanding, as it might be something very turbulent and traumatic that still gets you to the end goal. That end goal again is TRUTH.

Lets break down what truth actually is and if it is the same for us all in terms of belief. The ideas around universal truth and what it means to have a personal truth are vastly different and we want to make sure you understand that you do have personal freedom and choice. Personal truth is not the same for everyone, its an individual understanding. Universal truth is beyond that which can be different and what melds us together as one— such as being human. Don't allow anyone else dictate what your truths actually are because they are based in the way you perceive the world, the eyes you look through see's life in a way that is unique to you and your life experience.

A spiritual awakening journey is a path that is laid out by your own realizations of what feels important, the desires deep within your psyche, and reshaping the way you'd like your life to look. This path helps you decide who you are by helping you determine what you are not and miracles seem to occur as the path towards exposing this truth shines brighter with each step forward. Trusting this process in life allows you to follow your most authentic expression. Trust your unique path and have faith that they way things are unfolding is the way its supposed to happen for you, in the ways you truly need it to.

Affirmation For Connecting To Your Spiritual Awakening Journey:

"I know this road is special to my existence because I am here to shine, I am eternally grateful now that I understand at a deep level, that I am a magnet for miracles, and a good life. And so it is."

Chapter Two:
What is Energy?

Everything in the world contains energy and there are many different kinds to call upon depending on what you are in need of. Its important to understand that all of these energies have something very specific they do. Realizing that you can harness the power of multiple energies will give you freedom of choice and ultimate power over your experience.

Energies are an all knowing source of vibrational frequency that brings an individual to higher states of happiness or clarity. Energy also represents the things that we feel that have low vibrational frequency and can be considered of a negative connotation. Energies can sum up states we find ourselves in that either heighten our awareness for life and make it feel amazing, or we have those moments that make us feel low and ask us to rest.

Utilizing your energy in positive ways toward the future while you are in the present is one way to utilize energies at your own free will. There are affirmations and meditations provided if you feel you are lacking in any of these energetic categories or would like to harness more power in them, they can be found at the end of each section.

Spiritual Energy

What exactly is spiritual energy and what is it used for? Simply put, it is the energy you give when you are focused on love and pure being. When you are yourself, full of compassion for others and connected to the larger expression of life– the Universe. Spiritual Energy gives the ability to tap into something greater and can ultimately give someone a lot of meaning in their life. These energies can be found in totems like statues or photos of a beloved guru or family member and can include objects like jewelry or books like Bible. This energy when felt, brings an overwhelming sense of calm combined with feelings of well-being.

Another place that spiritual energy can be found is in spiritual places like the mountains of Himalayas where monks meditate and can include ashram's (spiritual centers), temples and churches. These can be any place of worship where the energy of the individual is brought to a sense of peace.

Spiritual energy is also the realization that there is something larger out in the world besides our personal experiences. Trusting or having faith in something outside of yourself gives meaning to circumstances and the will to press forward when a person find themselves in a difficult state.

Affirmation For Connecting To Your Spiritual Energy:

"I see and feel the energetic vibrations that shift my energy. It comes over me when I am full of love, positive thoughts and compassion for myself. May I connect to this feeling often. It is and so it will be."

Mental Energy

Mental energy is that which we call upon to give us the motivation to get up and move in life. It takes great effort to learn and to catalogue what we see in the world. Our mental energy is what helps us look at something and make sense of what's happening. This is the place that our reality lies as it is the place where we decide how we feel about what we see in front of us.

Mental energy can give us the strength to cognitively move forward with life because it is where our memories live and how we process information. The energy of the mind is such a strong faculty because its ability to compartmentalize, memorize, and recall is intrinsic and instinctual.

One overlooked quality about mental energy is that gets us ahead in life. It provides the keen ability to use the mind to manifest energy into what we desire and need out of life. This is where affirmations come to life and where the power of their use resides.

Mental energy must be looked at as a superpower, but not the only thing we rely on. There is an important need to harness and protect this energy by giving it some rest. Restful activities include meditation, staring at a beautiful object, drawing, sewing or making something intuitive with your hands. Lending yourself to these activities not only gives you a break from decision making or thinking about the past, present, or future, but helps you make better decisions when the moment arises. Spontaneous action or decision making can be from a place of calm resolve because you find ways to give yourself peace and avoid burn out from decision making.

Affirmation For Connecting To Your Mental Energy:

"I trust my mind when it is coupled with my heart, the intentions are always towards curiosity, understanding and connection to life. May my mind stay vital. May I remain free to access information that helps me grow. It is and so it will be."

Emotional Energy

Emotional Energy is an intelligent energy that takes a way a person feels and transforms it into a larger energy that can be felt by people who are also sensitive and in tune by being connected strongly to their personal emotional energy. Empathy lives here and is the feeling of absorbing the emotions of others or the collective feelings in a room. This is the energy used to understand on a deeper level why you operate the way you do– because you are a feeling human being who has emotions on just about everything.

Emotional energy for some is not an easy thing to control, some of us have been through so much in life that our emotional energy is large and intuitive, representing center of someone's whole life. Being sensitive to how you feel is what we call emotional intelligence and represents a very human, but important part of our life experience– feeling and responding to emotions.

Its not feminine or masculine to connect to your emotional energy, it's a balance of understanding when love is supposed to be present, its being aware enough to protect those emotions if needed, and worth expressing for a better, more expansive life. Taking care to protect these emotions and keep them healthy will require your intuitive inclinations about who you surround yourself with and what you deal with from day to day. Oftentimes you are not able to protect yourself if you work in customer service and are subject to other peoples moods or irritations. A lot of times we come from families that have not been supportive or nurturing towards our emotional energy and many of us unfortunately have no connection to this energy because there is an ingrained fear to get close to it.

This section is to remind you of its importance and why its okay to open up to its intelligence and allow the messages to come through, its okay to trust the way you feel, and it's a good idea to reach out to those you may have in your life that nurture this sentiment. If you don't have anyone physical to share this with, then Journaling and internalizing your experience may work for a small amount of time. After a while, you will need to be a part of a group, experience lively interaction and rejoice with others who are connected to their emotional energy and are not afraid to be.

Affirmation For Connecting To Your Emotional Energy:

"My emotional energy is in tune and represents heightened awareness of who I am. I am not afraid of my emotions or my connection to them. I will express my emotions when it is safe and comfortable to do so. It is and so it will be."

Physical Energy

Physical energy is the force that is stored within the muscles and tissues of the body. It is what we call upon when we need to get up from the couch or the energy exerted when exercising or playing with children. It is what you feel throughout your physicality that lets you know you are alive and able to move. We use this energy for many functions, but we don't often realize how to harness or sequester more of it.

Continuing high vibration frequencies requires a store of physical energy that is ready for spontaneous and dynamic movement, not bogged down by impurities of the mind or digestive system. Taking care of what you eat is an important factor in improving the quality and longevity of your physical energy. Considering your body type, location, and how you like to eat, its best to look for these things in the purest form you are able– raw or whole. Its also imperative that you consume foods either prepared in your home or made by someone you can actually see or know. When you know the person making your food or where the ingredients came from, there is a physical connection that cannot be matched by any other substance, in any other way. Taking care to consider where your food comes from automatically sets your physical energy up for success and it doesnt take much. If raw or whole foods seem hard to find in your area, frozen is the next best option as it contains more nutrient density than canned foods are able to offer.

Affirmation For Connecting To Your Physical Energy:

"My physical energy is important to me and I consciously take care to harness its power by giving my body what it needs and deserves. I care about myself physically, mentally, and spiritually. It is and so it will be."

Explaining Auras

Auras are energetic fields that can be sensed by highly sensitive people. Auras and their colors can reveal a meanings related to the way you feel and encase your whole body in a specific color that extends to the world and the people around what they can pick up from you and your energy.

An aura can be seen anywhere from 3 to 30 feet around your physical body. The closer to the body, the stronger and more intense the color can be seen. The further away, them more delicate and sensitive the color can look. This color is a representation of the true nature of a person when all habits and forms have been stripped away. It's the true nature without the superficial conditioning of today's society.

What Aura Colors say about a person

Orange: Represents creativity and everything that represents the Sacral chakra. It is the color of someone who has vibrant energy and is ready to take on the world with their creative pursuits. Emotional and spiritual balance can be counted on when you see the color orange around a person. This color represents a thoughtful person and someone who is sensitive to another individuals needs. There is a tendency to be overly ambitious or have a lack of will, so balance is needed in order to achieve a state of peace and equilibrium.

Pink: Represents love, healing and gratitude for life. When this color shows up for a person it can mean they feel loved and are loved deeply by someone in their immediate environment. If you run into a person like this, you may get an overwhelming sense of calm and trust in this person because they are ready to receive and offer truth.

Green: This color represents peace and harmony. This person will be or has been healing from issues of the past and is moving forward with their lives. There is a willingness to be there for other people and offer a lending ear or help when its truly needed. This person is compassionate and settled in themselves. Sometimes this color can lead to feelings of jealousy and envy, so it is important to be happy with what is happening in your life and continue to go your own way.

Blue: This is a color of tranquility and spiritual pursuits. This person will be in their creativity centers trying their best to understand the larger meanings of life and how to move forward. These people can be sensitive and loyal, providing the presence needed to be a good friend and confidant. Oftentimes these kind souls experience mood swings and feelings of uncertainty, but over time, their introspection has them moving on with grace.

Yellow: Happiness, patience and self control. This color offers self control to a persons awareness. They realize they create their own reality and optimism meets them where they are. These friendly people understand their circumstance and offer patience and calm happiness to a situation when the need for it comes along. Sometimes these people can find themselves in a place they didn't intend to be, they are encouraged to not follow too anyone else's flow of life and to follow their own direction pull.

Red: vitality survival. This is the color of someone who is strong and has seperated themselves from the status quo. You know you can count on these people to show up in life with a firey demeanor that offers strength and a passion towards new adventures. This highly energized and sexual color gives a superpower to its muse– pushing past fear.

Grey: These people may often seem depressive or cold to the touch. You can tell they are not getting enough sleep and are lacking a sense of love in their life. They may often come off as negative or tired and its because they have been working so hard to figure out how to return back to homeostasis. These people are in need of love and reminders of just how special they are in the world. It may take them time to remember, but these are the people that need our help without them needing to ask. If you see this color for yourself, its wise to connect with positive people that help you see the value of your worth.

Brown: This color will often represent a person who seems absent minded and just not "there". They will often be in their own minds trying to determine what is fact and what is fiction. Greed sometimes presents itself because it is hard for this color to look past personal led desires and goals. Its wise to take patience when this color comes up and to take opinions or negative thought patterns with a grain of salt.

Indigo: This is the color of a seeker, a person who above all else, moves with the way of the spirit and goes toward trying to understand how they are part of the ALL, oneness, The Universe. You will notice the integrity of these people to be high and their intuition to be off the charts. These are great people to go to for advice and can always lend words that come from benevolence, love and compassionate understanding.

White: This color is a full representation of perfect balance and purity. It's a color you may not see often or you may, but generally seen on children and those who hold high spiritual stature in the world. This is a person you can trust and will be able to receive you with no internal led motivations or goals.

Black: This color lacks depth, life, and love. This is the color of death or when someone has turned over to the other side– continued darkness. Its wise to not be alarmed when you see this color as it doesn't necessarily mean that this person will die, but they are experience a death of sorts. It could be a death of ego, disillusionment or abuse. Treat them with kindness and protect your energy as best as possible. If this color is showing up for you and around you, its wise to look inside and take stalk of what has changed and what will be sparked to grow in its place.

Energy Work

Energy work is the physical practice that works to facilitate and environment and experience of health and healing by re-aligning the bodies energies and bodily energetic centers (chakras). This work can also encompass energetic work that does not require physical touch like reading auras, but the sensations remain the same. People oftentimes report feelings of overall happiness and well-being increase, tingling sensations in the temples, rushing and flooding of the bodies release of emotions. Reiki, Chakra Balancing and hands on healing are just a few modalities that belong to energy work.

Energetic work is a skill sometimes realized by the practitioner before being trained. They see there is a drive and ambition to be close to or help people who need the energy you have to give. Oftentimes these people will pick up on their gifts and look for people who can help them channel the skill with more precision and give more value to the people they help. Energetic work has been performed by human beings for centuries by using the bodies frequencies and a healers touch, to move the energy in a persons body towards balance and wholeness.

Energy Medicine

Energy medicine is one of the oldest forms of healing known to man. Before there were fancy pills that fixed our common ailments and issues, medicine people used the magic of energy medicine to nurse their communities back to health. Many traditions across the world practice and integrate energy healing from ancient tradition. Some of which include, Acupuncture, Shamanism, Reflexology, Reiki, Cranial Sacral Healing and so much more.

The reasons people visit energy healers to receive energy medicine can range from the following: Needing help with grief, loss in the family, headaches, emotional upheavals, abuse, trauma, sleep and increased need for protection. People often report simple, yet rewarding benefits by opening their minds and hearts to the healing powers of energy medicine. Reduced anxiety is one the stark realizations because the sense of calm and grounding can bring a person back to center. This work can include healing but is not limited to, connecting to one's inner self, mental clarity and fortitude, better memory and increased sleep as well as a decrease in chronic pain a person can experience. With regular visits to qualified individuals, the more helpful benefits can be achieved.

Tantric Energy

Tantric energy is the essence that is comprised of a spiritual science dating back more than 5,000 years ago and encompasses the flow and energy of breath work, yogic contortions and sexual energetic exchange. Tantra means the matrix itself, everything in the universe mixed together to formulate a web, and everything is connected to this web of life. Tantra is not just the practice of having sex, it is much more of a connective experience for both people where they have the opportunity to enjoy breath and physical sensations in the body that arouse and bring a person to a state of bliss. Release with this person may never come, but the action of holding out, being present and asking for what you need mentally while in communion with another is key to enjoyment and understanding. This tradition is considered a science and not a religion or something you must follow for purity.

Chapter Three:
All About Chakras

The Chakra's and energy centers of the body are the most important to understand and grasp because they give so much confidence, reasoning, and compassion towards the human experience. The locations, colors, and motivations of these nodules of energy give a person many opportunities to understand the meaning of their personal journey. Many don't know about these areas of the body, so when something comes to a crisis, its often hard to deal with because the source has not been located. Proper healing techniques and ceremonies of the past are not being utilized due to the lost art of knowing these teachings and many years of disconnecting from our roots.

The 7 Chakras

The 7 Main Inner Chakras are explained below in great detail. Its to be understood that the 7 main inner chakras carry a wealth of knowledge, are some of the easiest to connect to and heal with. It is like having a rainbow inside of your body starting at the base of your body and working its way up through the head. These are the most widely known and practiced around the world and finding more of their magical properties and uses are not hard to find.

The First Chakra– The Root

The Sanskrit name for this chakra is called the Mooladhara, Moola means the root and the place where all the other chakra's lay. It is when someone uses this book, studies ancient scriptures, asks deeper questions, develops a practice, and realizes they want more out of a relationship than just physical contact. It is awakened though long times of being by oneself, taking up a devoted spiritual practice or are enticed to learn more about your inner workings. The First chakra is where the serpent energy has coiled within each of us 3 and a half times, waiting for the chance to learn, grow, and help us transcend into another place. The goal is to obtain a level of consciousness that drives progress and to moves us past the lower energies life brings us. The First chakra is where everything begins and cannot move to the other chakras until this one has been discovered and completely opened.

This chakra stores all of our trauma, pain from the past, passion, desire, and deep rooted fears. This is the chakra where we learn to control our sexual impulses to transcend to the next stage and evolve– one does not have to renounce it all together. The purpose is to utilize the energy of release by working avidly to manifest what you need out of life. The location of this chakra is different for male parts then it is for female parts. For the male parts, the Root is located at the perineum between the anus and sexual organ. For females this energy center lies in the area of the cervix. These areas are

47

responsible for giving birth, waking up to purpose, and the fight or flight response.

When you are working with your Root chakra, you can experience the lowest energies of human existence. While alcohol, partying, and long nights out on the town feel invigorating and stimulating to participate in, when we stay here in these activity, our Root lays dormant or in a state of sleep. In high states of emotional upheaval and toxins, the energy is not able to move forward, heal, or digest what's happening to them or for them. When you are full of negative actions and reactions, you can experience lack and the feelings of being stagnant in the Root chakra.

This area of the body is mentioned to be an area of emotional upheaval and deep pain. It is the place where greed, anger, stress, and jealousy lye within the body. When this area is brought to life, enhanced emotions and feelings will arise and with increased frequency. At the core these feelings stem from knowing there is something missing that either comes from having very little as a child or experiencing extreme hardship or trauma– which encompasses a vast amount of human beings. Not having your basic needs met, resource scarcity, void of nurturing, and not having access to the tools needed for healthy emotional development. When you are in a constant state of survival or autopilot, you forget about your needs and old patterns begin to show up again. Working diligently with this chakra will allow repeat patterns to finally make their way out of your life.

Affirmation For The Root Chakra:

"May I continue this journey of healing by leveling up my emotional maturity, whatever that needs to look like for me. I am strong in my conviction to heal the centers of my body. And so it is".

The Second Chakra– Sacral Chakra

The Sanskrit name for this chakra is Swadhisthana, swa meaning "ones own" and adhisthana meaning "dwelling place". It is where a person uses the power of their first chakra and examines where the root issues stem from. The second chakra is the place where a person owns their emotions and personal expression in life. The second chakra is involved with the first chakra because they both the catalyst for awakening the whole system. The lower two inner chakra's are hardest to penetrate and need a major mental and physical breakthroughs to move the energy up the spine and higher states of being.

The symbolism is a 6-Petaled orange colored lotus that connects us with the element of water and the ebbs and flows of the Moons cycles. It connects us to emotion whether we are conscious of why it has come up or what the emotion is. The energy of this chakra relates to the way we personalize our lives, our sense of security, and how we soothe ourselves emotionally. This area of our bodies also represents comfort and a stable sense of home and family. Some women may experience heightened sensitivity and heavy menstrual cycles and both sexes may experience dull or lifeless orgasm as this energy finally reaches a state of awakening.

Many emotions lay dormant in the first and second chakras of the body because it holds many lifetimes of problems that you and your Soul mates been working improving and moving past. Working on healing this area of life and the body is by sticking close to the Moons lunation cycles– the waxing and waning of a new moon and full moon inquiries are just one way to connect and observe how you function in between the two week cycle from one to the next.

This is the place of unconscious patters and places that store the many memories of hurt. It is here where we compartmentalize our problems for the sake of getting through life.

When working with the Second chakra can look like a person who is really trying to understand the details of their life. You will be paying attention to the sudden feelings of change and you will be able to tune into energies on a very subtle level. Patterns in life will make themselves noticeable so you are able to actively change them if you choose. The work of digging deep into the psyche to pull out some semblance of healing grace.

This is the chakra of love, sex, and money. This is where we "hunger for more" and where we start to identify our material needs and desires. This chakra gives you the motivation to work more towards the physical and less thought or action toward the spiritual realm can be experienced.

Affirmation For The Sacral Chakra:

"I am ready to understand more of my core desires and step up where my energy feels best served. And so it is".

The Third Chakra– Solar Plexus

The third chakra is the place where the action starts to begin, where one starts to control the intensity with how fast they move and progress forward. This chakra controls our projection and breathing process through the diaphragm. It is here the hammer of the navel pounds against the front of the spine to move the lungs and increase breath or "prana" within the body– Yogic Breathing technique called Fire Breath. Buddhist traditions point to this being where the Kundalini Awakens, not the Root chakra. Because it is where consciousness begins to evolve and blossom.

The Sanskrit name for this chakra is Manipura, Mani meaning "jewel" and Pura meaning "city". It is where one takes the energy of the First 2 Chakra's and its foundations to identify where one will start to direct their life in a conscious way. The city of jewels is exactly what it means. When working with the Navel, the breath, prana, we become the driver of the cleansing and clearing of the mind through intentional breathing.

Symbolism- the 10-Petaled Lotus and connects with the element of Fire and the natural ebb and flow of the Suns cycles. It connects us to what we actually intend to do with our lives, the proper steps and practices that lead to more energy and opportunity to develop the steps. The Element of Fire burns up what no longer serves, reducing physical or mental matter into ashes– easily able to blow away in the wind. Fire is the ferocity the propels a person to take one more step in a marathon. It can be to cry harder about what moves a person by rapidly moving the belly as deep sobs drive the feeling more intently. It is where the loudness of one's voice resides.

The Location of the third chakra is between the naval and the anterior part of the spine. It's the area of our body that contains the kidneys, bladder, digestive tract, metabolism, and is the body temperature control system. This is the part of the body where it gets strangely clear that you are what you think you are. If you think you are a terrible dancer, then well, you will be. If you are determined to be a doctor or writer and believe you are before it happens gives you the gusto to continue moving. The Navel is the center that starts to stir the magic of manifestation and breathing through and to the new life you are working to experience.

Affirmation For The Solar Plexus Chakra:

"When I focus on the breath, I focus on my life force and I become the most powerful version of myself. And so it is".

The Fourth Chakra– The Heart Chakra

The fourth chakra is the place where open hearted compassion lies. Its where we deeply connect with the emotional energy and how we discover in the end– to love people despite what they have done. We never have to consider the automatic nature of the heart. It opens up and exposes itself to danger for the sake of feeling love and appreciation from other's. It can also create a shield of protection, but also keeping you stuck in the lower centers of the body, if you are unable to shed and open.

The Sanskrit name for this chakra is Anahata meaning "un-struck", the continuous beat of the heart does it consistently and in an unbroken rhythm. It's the place in our body that protects our feelings or makes us a beacon for interactions that bring more joy through the expansion of love. This chakra awakens the Air element, clearing the way for joyous disposition, a logical approach, easy controlled breathing and an oneness to refine inner processing. Awakening the Air process in the body came from the mastery of the Naval through breath work. Digestion of what's occurred to you, the traumas or tensions that reside in your body gets processed through Air and the metronome of the heart. The location of this Chakra encompasses not only the heart, but the lungs as well.

A beneficial and safe way to tap into the powerful force behind the heart chakra is to be in nature, connecting to all to all of the color green you can, again, the idea is to remove yourself from your personal environment and to experience the vastness around you. Take in scenery that makes your heart swell with joy and happiness. If this is not accessible for you, it is recommended you connect to the scenery you do have access to whether it be digital, photographs or video chats with friends in places that can help you connect. You are never limited by your circumstance, location, race, gender, identification, or sexual orientation. We utilize the tools we have in the spaces we were given to work with and prove once again that the Kundalini lives and moves inside of each and every one of us, no matter what kind of life we were born into.

Being in the heart and having this activation brings about a lot situations and feel like they need to be forgiven or that you need to increase your compassion for the people involved instead of holding tight to your previous beliefs. You may find yourself reaching out to people you haven't spoken to in ages, willing to rebuild bridges of friendship and finally putting to bed all the expectation that led to disappointment. You may realize that holding on to emotions doesn't serve who you truly are.

Affirmation For The Heart Chakra:

"When I focus on the breath, I focus on my life force and I become the most powerful version of myself. And so it is".

The Fifth Chakra– The Throat Chakra

The fifth chakra brings truth, its less about what you say and more about what you intuitively sense. The Throat chakra is where voice is established and what is projected to others. Its speaking up for yourself and being able to ask questions to clarify your understanding. Its also the place where you speak who you are through the environments you live in.

The Sanskrit name is the Vishuddhi chakra, shuddhi meaning to purify, this chakra stands for purification. It is through purification one can ensure they are speaking from their true selfand are coming from a place of inner knowing. You end up changing your words when purification is present and you choose language that accurately represents your experience. Purification lends itself to words, what are you no longer willing to say out loud because its no longer true for you? Who are you no longer willing to talk about because it doesn't make you feel good? What will you make vocal to others about what you will tolerate and what you can no longer put up with?

The location of the throat chakra is behind the the voice box and includes everything around the jaw line, neck, and shoulders. This part of our body takes in nutrients in the form of food and is where our tonal vibration lies. Not all sustenance is in the form of something you take in through the mouth, it does include what you allow others to say to you and what you are able to pick up on in your environment.

The things you hear, taste, touch, smell and talk about will all suddenly change and the people around you will not only take notice, but start to inquire about how to get what it is you have. Waiting until you are asked not only instills your authority because you look like a person who knows, but you savor the moments of explaining what it is you know–finally! People will be mesmerized because the tone of your voice and the development of the throat begins to mature like that of a wisdom keeper. This chakra gives you your intrinsic power because if you could not exercise your voice, your thoughts or your ideas, you would not feel heard and it would be hard to connect to others.

Affirmation For The Throat Chakra:

"I intend to speak my mind and be in my truth at all times. And so it is".

The Six Chakra– The Third Eye

The Sixth chakra is the space between the middle of the brow. However its actual location resides at the top of the spine and can be said to represent the Eye of Shiva. It is located in the area of our head where sight beyond sight occurs.

The Sanskrit name is the Ajna chakra, Ajna meaning "to know, to obey or to follow" and is faithfully known as the "Guru chakra" because of its intuition enhancing abilities. What's meant by this is an understanding that there is a higher power at work to help guide you to happiness. You obey or follow the directions of the inner self to get to higher planes of thinking and better ways of living a quality life.The symbolism of this chakra is a 2 petaled lotus with a circle in the middle and is a physical representation of the eyes. However this eye in the middle is not exactly opened outward, instead its closed focusing on the being within– staring at the Soul to see what it needs next.

When there is a goal to life and a focus on the picture outside of self gratification, opportunities to be of service, materials needed to start the project begin to surface, and the people needed to network help you connect the missing links. It leads you to people like yourself who have similar goals, while some of these groups will be small, the impact is what matters most. The value of this chakra is pertinent to self improvement and knowing oneself fully. When you are focused and centered within you care less about what others are doing and more about how you will get to the higher points of life, the more you will try to experience for yourself and the more you begin to make yourself an autonomous entity– enjoying time alone and contemplating /manifesting the life you wish to continue.

It can really show itself as innumerable possibilities, the idea is to allow the process to unfold for without expectation. Having these kinds of sights will not feel scary or overwhelming if you are activated to take it on. Slow down if you feel as if this process increases ideation's that may not seem like yours. You ultimately want the decisions you make and the thoughts you think to be your own. Listening to yourself is of great importance.

Taking care to allow this chakra to blossom as it needs to involves rigorous practice and dedication. Mantra Yoga or a devout Meditation practice are some of the best remedies to keep this eye focused within. Mantra Yoga will have you concentrate on spiritual words, and allowing you to ask for the blessings of the spirit you believe in, God/Goddess, deity, Buddha, or the Universe. Mediation is another way to nurture the quieting of the mind and gives you the positive reinforcement that its okay to be where you are in the moment. With the stimulation of the Third Eye purpose, drive and a sense of individuality becomes more wholly centered. You always want the opportunity to be yourself and give the world what it is you think it should have from you– nothing more.

Affirmation For The Third Eye Chakra:

"When I focus on the person within, I realize who I am in each moment. It is, and so it will be".

The Seventh Chakra– The Crown Chakra

The seventh chakra is the place where the feminine and masculine finally meet at the top of the head. It is the complete and total Awakening of the Kundalini and all its faculties. From the Root chakra to the Third Eye, everything is pushed past just an activation or stimulation of the chakra's.

The Sanskrit name is the Sahasrara chakra the "one thousand" an is to represent the nadis (energetic loops) that wrap around the entire body and helping the central wiring system (nervous system) stay alert and on command as a high intelligence that helps you navigate the world and to feel comfortable while doing it.

The location of this chakra is on the top of the head, liken its location to the soft spot of a newborn skull. It is a physical representation of as above, so below. What happens out there, happens in here. It's the connection between the physical body and the portal to the ethereal. What happens for a person beyond this measure is said to be of 7 higher spiritual centers that connect a person more with heaven, God, the Universe, The All, it's a recognition that there is something out there, beyond you, your thinking, your experiences, and your sight. With that said, the varying degrees of what can happen for and to a person can only become clear as more people experience the phenomena of Awakening there own Kundalini– a natural born right to those on the path.

The Crown chakra is to bring back the memory that nothing is outside of yourself. The internal motivation it takes to lead yourself down a road of resourcefulness comes from the personal need to make it so. If nothing is outside of yourself than love is not something you need from others, its enough for you to give love to yourself, love is inside of you. When you have reached this center and are working with the activation of this chakra, happiness comes effortlessly and the spread of this feeling is contagious. The Crown chakra is the connection to a vast system of knowledge, intuition, and spiritual understanding. It is the area that connects us to the higher realms of heaven

Affirmation For The Crown Chakra:

"I am full of wholeness and love as equilibrium and balance bless me. Its is and so it will be".

Chakra Colors
First Chakra
The color red represents its animalistic value on your system, the instinctual parts of our psyche, why we rise, get angry, or want to fight. Red is the color of strength, war, the blood that runs through our veins and the signal we need to push the break peddle. It represents the fire inside that sends us on

a journey to something new, burning away all that held us hostage.

Second Chakra
The color of this chakra is orange representing the blending of the lower center (the Root) and the chakra center ahead of it (the Navel)– the red root and yellow navel make an orange Sacral chakra. To help work through the blockages of this energetic center you must utilize what comes up from the foundation of your life and utilize the breath to work through the emotional upheavals.

Third Chakra
The color of the third chakra is represented by the color Yellow, another visual connection to the Sun, the color gold and the symbolism of power, drive, and strength. This is why it can be known under another pseudonym– The Solar Plexus. The Sun represents our creativity and the ability to derive the self confidence needed to create what needs to be shared with our communities. It's the first sense in realizing what you love is connected to a bigger sense, the individual nature of a person begins to take a more objective approach. Being able to see why we do the things we do and how to make it less about me and more about us. When we take the focus off our own personal attainment, we start working towards the service of others and what your specific gifts offer that make the world go around. Many adjustments are made with this chakra and may be the longest one to get through for some.

Fourth Chakra

The color of this chakra is Green as it represents new growth and understanding. Like the Spring flowers that bloom every April, so does the heart as it slowly unfolds revealing the center of its universe. It is a color to remind you of what represents hope and what connects us to the land we reside in, the foods we choose and the lively loving Soul's we find ourselves attracted to. It's the color of being able to move forward and what we look for when selecting particular vegetables to eat. It's the color of abundance and the budding of higher states of consciousness.

Fifth Chakra

The color of this chakra is Blue representing the vast open sky's that cover all of the world and the depths of oceans and seas below it. What remains in the middle of these vast bodies is a reality that is removed from ego and more connected to the wholeness. This lotus with 16-petals gives a person the power to move with conviction and ease as parts of a person settle, anger becomes a chuckle, sadness becomes contemplation, and heaviness turns into a time of self care. This is what it means to understand who you are and what you can and cannot change about yourself–it softens the spirit and increases vocabulary.

Sixth Chakra

The color of this chakra is Indigo a represents a color that is not commonly seen, but is recognized as magnificence when it is seen. It is a color of blue

that offers a vibrancy and state of well-being and
that is a close comparison to the chakra itself, as
many who try to attain this awakening loose sight
and need reminders, this color will offer that. There
are the desert people of Tuareg people who shine
brightly in the Sun with Indigo materials draped
over their bodies. Bright, happy, devoted people
who take the situation they are presented and not
only thrive while doing it, but make it absolutely
beautiful. It's a color that represents Royal or
Imperial bloodline and is one of the true colors of
staying connected to your ancestral roots– feeling
and seeing the intuitive practices, preparing elixirs,
spontaneous body movements, and ceremonies you
have internal access to, but maybe were not trained
in.

Seventh Chakra
The color of this chakra is Violet, representing the
periodical colors of spring and summer that show
an individual what it means to be alive. This color
can be seen behind the eyes when in deep
meditative states. This color is the sign of
enlightenment and union with the self. It is the
fullness of understanding and the practice of the
Kundalini– self-study. This color can be worn or
furnished to remind you of the vastness outside of
your experience and the pure energy that emanates
from you because of you diligent Yogic practice
and focus toward the inward journey of self
knowledge.

Chapter Four:
Relearning Self-Love

Around the globe human beings strive to find a symbiotic existence with the immediate world that surrounds us. We look for a reflection of ourselves that feels good to us, either through self judgement or by accepting the judgement of those around us. Whether we find our connection through religion, social interaction, self-reflective practices, or through physical activities such as sports- there is a relentless need to find cohesion and comradery with others on this journey of being Human.

Most religions seek to show the way by highlighting the need to give up limited human "control" to something greater than self. By doing this, we become a part of something larger and fulfill our human need of being an integral piece of the group. We human beings are social creatures and desire mental, physical and emotional connections in our daily lives to give us meaning and purpose. To exist with neither meaning nor purpose is destructive to the human psyche.

In Buddhism the higher power dwells within- a level of self that already exists and only needs to be accessed or discovered. In Christianity, Christians strive to overcome human weakness by submitting personal control over to a benevolent God that is all knowing and definitely better at navigating the pitfalls and hurdles of life. God is the consciousness that created everything, so who better to trust. This thereby relieves the mind and spirit of the burdens that seem to befall humans. New Age beliefs aim to find this same comfort in something greater than self through the power of clear, positive thinking and maintaining higher spiritual vibrations. In this way the ability to align with the energies larger than the human self allow an ease and symbiosis with life. The same follows for most other religions even though the specifics and practices differ.

At the core of these beliefs is a fundamental knowledge that on some level we humans tend to get in our own way. That if by releasing our fears to something more powerful, we may then be able to actually enjoy the lives that we are living, not just survive to get through them. This concept points out the lack of expansive foresight involved with human decision making. If we are able to get over ourselves- literally and figuratively- we will be able to ascend to higher states of being and have a most fulfilling life.

Because of a perceived higher level of consciousness- mainly the ability to verbally process and express feelings- human behavior is deemed to be about more than just mere survival. On all continents Anthropologists have spent centuries uncovering, then speculating on the behaviors and motivations of countless primitive societies in an effort to connect homosapiens to the humans of today. By attempting to show our shared motivations through things like cave art, musical instruments and pottery, scientists demonstrate that ancient humans are more than "mere animals".

According to verywell.com "The time line of psychology spans centuries, with the earliest known mention of clinical depression in 1500 BCE on an ancient Egytian manuscript known as the Ebers Papyrus...it was not until the 11th century that the persian physician Avicenna attributed a connection between emotions and physical responses in a practice dubbed psychological psychology..." They go on to state that Sigmund Freud began offering therapy to patients in 1886, that being the "official" beginning of what is termed modern psychology.

From Jung and Freud to Iyanla Vanzant and Deepak Choppra, working to discover our darkest secrets is the very basis of psychological healing. There are too many exercises, techniques and systems to name here but for even the most introspective and courageous individuals transversing the gauntlet of self work is extremely difficult. There are many layers to the personas that we spend a lifetime cultivating. These layers are being continually added as we experience life and it is beneath these layers that we discover who we truly are by dissecting what we have been through.

Our actions are dictated by the decisions that we make and these decisions are made consciously, subconsciously/unconsciously ie. known to us or unknown to us. The way that the human mind works to decipher then decide seems a very conscious activity, but according to a slide show released by the Mayo Clinic "How the Brain Works", "A complicated highway system of nerves connects your brain to the rest of your body, so communication occurs in split seconds...While all parts of your brain work together, each part is responsible for a specific function- controlling everything from your heart rate to your mood."

There are so many components that work in conjunction to move this vehicle we call a human body. According to the same slide show, the four parts of the human brain- frontal lobes, parietal lobes, occipital lobes and temporal lobes work in unison and function at the speed of light. The brain has two sides and each side contains the following;

*The frontal lobes control thinking, planning, organising, problem solving, short term memory and movement.
*The parietal lobes interpret sensory information, sucha s taste, temperature and touch.
*The occipital lobes process images from your eyes and link that information with images stored in the memory.
*The temporal lobes process information from your senses of smell, taste and sound. They also play a role in memory storage.

Multiple studies have been done to locate where in the human brain the actual "command center" is. In the article "A Triple Dissociation of Neural Systems Supporting the ID, EGO, and SUPEREGO" written by Steven Z. Fisher, 1,2*+ Stephen T. Student 1,2+-, an MRI study was done with seven nineteen year old males, with common backgrounds. The subjects were asked a series of questions as images and recordings catalogued the neural activity. The information was analyzed to differentiate where in the brain certain responses originate. The conclusion showed that the "EGO related neural activity was centered on the anterior cingulate cortex...no other region of the brain." The cingulate cortex is located in the limbic lobe, a layer between the four lobes listed above and the thalamus.

Psychology likens the ego to computer software- a foundational set of commands that runs our decision making, the actions we take in our lives and the emotions that come as a result. The origin of the word ego is Latin and simply means "I". It is used commonly today thanks to the work of Sigmund Freud. According to Freud "the ego is the component of personality that is responsible for dealing with reality." Basically, the ego is how we see ourselves as we move through the world, an internal mirror of who we think we are. When developing his psychoanalytic theory, Freud used his native German word es- meaning "it". However when the work was being translated the translator decided to use the word ego in its place.

The human personality or ego, has been informed by external influences from the moment of consciousness. Studies have shown the first seven years of a person's life are the most crucial to cognitive health and emotional development. These are the years that our personality or ego, is the most informed and transformed. The image of a clear untouched canvas seems most apropos, once an artist begins creating, the canvas can no longer return to its original untouched state.

For most of us these formative years are spent in close proximity to our primary caretakers. Children are essentially sponges, and these first seven years are the years of being an untouched canvas. They are absorbed in what is happening in the world that surrounds them. According to psychology theory the brain takes in information and catalogues it mentally as well as emotionally and these beginning years are where emotional and cognitive foundations are laid- all decisions and emotional responses are thereafter affected by these primary moments.

For most people this original "software" can seem to have flaws. With all information having been taken in or "imprinted" during these first years of life, there can seem to be a division between how we have been programmed to function and something underneath that feels more true to who we feel we are. For some, there can definitely seem to be "two sides" to their ego.

On one hand there is the persona that is most known by those around us. For example, many people follow the rules set in place by their caretakers and society at large. They follow the rules, behave according to their cultural and societal norms and participate in the environment in ways that allow them to maneuver more easily. On the other hand, there is the person deep down inside that is hidden and protected from others. This is the part of ourselves that is the most vulnerable- who we are when we are alone.

Regardless of an individuals life experience, the ego influences how we move through the world, continue to take in information and how we respond to situations- be it "positively or negatively." Moments of vulnerability live with us, directly affecting the way we perceive the world and how we function in it.

The ego, this base or foundational software, functions like any software. It continues to function within the parameters of its original purpose until it is programmed to behave differently. Like software the ego is over writable and can be augmented to improve function and enhance peak performance. The human challenge lies in overwriting the portions of software that are so firmly rooted in the psyche that even when corrupted they are indistinguishable from the present reality. These are the portions of our motivations that dwell beneath the surface in our unconsciousness and function as if they are our original thoughts and actions.

For most of the commands that have been uploaded and live in our ego software, we are unaware of the moment that the commands were acquired. We remember incidents and the way that we reacted to them. We remember sweaty palms, and flushed faces, the color of the shirt we were wearing and that our best friend Suzie Callister had on green Converse.

What we don't realize is that this moment is not the actual "original" augment to our program. Far deeper beneath the layers may be something far more traumatic but less available to our conscious mind. The color green reminds you of an apron that your mother wore when you were a small child. In the pocket of that green apron you mother always kept a handful of red, cellophane plastic wrapped strawberry candies, and depending on whether the memory is positive or negative for you, it shapes your reaction to Suzie and her pair of green Converse.

If your mother rewarded you for a chore well done with one of those red candies from the pocket of her green apron, then the memory may very well bring about a warm feeling in your chest and a smile to your face. But if your mother taunted you with those small red wrapped strawberry candies by not offering you one or telling you that you did not deserve one even though you straightened your play area without being asked to, well then the memory associated with that color green may be negative to your psyche and brings about a trauma response.

In both scenarios the part of you that stores the memory does so without being consciously told to do so. Susie Callister's green shoes are just a pair of green shoes. She is your elementary school friend and you eat lunch with her everyday. Depending on your reaction to her shoes that day the dynamic of your friendship could be forever changed. Are we able to understand why we are feeling a particular way at seven years old? Do we even associate the color green of our best friends shoes to memories that are already years old?

Much like the apps that continually run in the background of your laptop or cellphone, your original ego software continues to run as it has been programmed to. So now at twenty eight, you are sitting in a cozy restaurant across from the person you love dearly and hope to spend the rest of your life with. They pull a small box from their pocket and place it on the table in front of them. This is the moment you have been waiting for, they are going to officially and romantically ask you if you would like to join them in marriage. But behind them an older woman sits facing you, she shares the table with an elderly gentleman. Her dress is the same shade of green as your mother's apron.

Your reaction may be more subtle than that day on the playground with your friend Susie Callister. You may notice that a certain feeling takes over your body, or you may not. You may be filled with loving warmth at the memory of your mother's slight dishwater damp hands unwrapping the small red candy for you. Or, you may be thoroughly repulsed by the sight of the dress and over taken by longing for the acceptance you never received. If the memory is a positive one, then the moment will be filled with an extra layer of "specialness". Your mother may have passed away and the sight of the color leaves you feeling as if she is giving you her blessing for a happy marriage. On the other hand, if your memories are unpleasant then you may receive the sight of the green dress as an omen or warning and the evening turns out very differently than what both of you had hoped.

Nothing has changed, it is the software that needs upgrading. The ego is only doing its job. Although now it is a bit outdated, the software is performing as the original inputting intended. Yes, years have passed but that foundational beginning layer has now permeated all aspects of your life. Any and all subsequent memories have been piled on top of it- including the playground moment with your best friend Susie Callister and her green Converse shoes. These layers are all embedded in the software of the ego.

Forgetting the Ego

This is where "forgetting the ego" becomes imperative. We must disconnect from the emotions and life experiences that have made you who you are, but often this is all but impossible. What you are attempting to do is move past the parts of the original software that are outdated and corrupted. It is time to discover what is true to who you are now.

This is a monumental feat. There are many parts of yourself that you are unaware of, Moments that have been imprinted into your memory that only surface in the presence of trauma. And although there is some awareness as to things you have been taught in your childhood, you mey be quite unaware of the original software altogether.

Things we like and those we dislike come into question. Do you really not like the color green? Or is there some traumatic event that has been buried deep within your psyche that presents as dislike or disdain. Do you really dislike family gatherings? Or did your uncle John behave so terribly on your third birthday that your family decided to no longer celebrate with the family and now you associate birthday cake with the dissolution of your familial gatherings.

There must be a separation made between the ego "I" or es, as Freud intended to call "it", the software that supports who we really are on the inside and who we are working to become. The work it takes to dislodge who we truly are from who our parents, society, our friends, our culture and the systems that support those ideologies, can be daunting at the very least. But take heart it can be done if taken in manageable portions and approached from the attitude that this is life long work and there are definitely no quick fixes. Impatience is the ruination of all of the work that you are doing to forget the ego.

When moving towards trying to dissolve your ego there are definite goals to keep in mind. Are you prepared to catch yourself when you fall? Because you will fall, everyone does when they attempt to dismantle all that they have known about themselves. There are moments when you will fantasize about what now feels like a simpler time in your life-even if those times were traumatic. Moments when the world around you had clear rules of engagement and you were more sure of the role you were to play, even if you were miserable.

You will most definitely miss the people, familiarity and support systems that reinforce the person you are currently trying to work on and leave behind, even if those people are still physically present in your life. The self examination that is needed to differentiate between your own needs and wants and the needs and wants of others will have you analyzing your closest relationships and the people you hold dear.

Because there are rare occasions when the "you" you wish to align with is the same "you" that everyone else is used to, there must be a realistic knowing that you may have to venture into this without your current support system. This does not mean that you will lose everyone that you have ever loved, but it points towards the realization that for a lot of people the person they present to the world is but a shadow of the person they truly are.

The work of forgetting the ego is a mental and physical journey. This work must absolutely be done by you and you alone. Others do not live in your mind, thus they are only aware of the parts of yourself that you chose to share. Understandably until you figure out what you need for you and your newly reprogrammed ego, there may be some lonely moments.

Dismantling who you have "always been" is life-long work. Many people have navigated the gauntlet of a rough adolescence and made it to adulthood and are fortunate to thrive in the lives that they have created for themselves. They are successful, have loving friends and family and typically appreciate the abundance they have cultivated in their lives. But somewhere deep down inside they are falling short of what makes them feel whole and there is a threshold that presents itself. The threshold presents through concentrated personal effort or when a person "chooses" not to pursue the dismantling of their ego and the change is promoted through the subconscious.

Attachments and Bonds

Who am I really? This is a fundamental question that we ask ourselves at some point in our lives. The depth the question is intended to dig to is up to the asker, but at its core the question is searching for personal meaning and direction. In past centuries, a person's life was more easily defined because life choices were limited. You were confined to your station according to things like gender, age and geographical location. Now with the advent of the Web, gender non-conforming breakthroughs and gender fluid occupations there is more choice as to how a person wants to live their life. Now more than ever before in human history it is easier to move around the world and explore the possibilities of your dreams.

We will use the fictional life and possible life choices of Caden to itterate our points from here forward. Caden is a seventeen year old male from a small mid-western United States town. He needs to decide what he wants to do upon graduating from high school. His father runs their family farm, he is a third generation farmer. His mother fills a traditional role as stay at home farmers wife.

Caden's upbringing has been very traditional. He is a typical teenager. He is smart and personable, polite and creative. He played the drums in the school band and likes science fiction books and movies. He is having a hard time deciding whether or not he should leave his hometown, his parents and his friends to go away to school.

But what if Caden secretly really wants to be a clothing designer in New York? What if Caden''s upbringing dictates that he stay in his hometown and take over the family business? He feels as if there is a responsibility to his family and that his parents have maintained the family farm with the intention of passing it down to future generations. Have they already decided what his future will be?

Had they decided for him even before he was born? And if that is what Caden's parents want for him, do we suppose that they will continually talk about taking his over the "farm one day" in hopes that the message buries deep in his psyche so deeply that he will eventually assume it has been his idea all along? Even before we understand language or hold our own heads up, we are fed someone else's dreams for us that we come to accept as our own.

The question of seeking out higher education or maybe moving to New York to study fashion is not the "right" decision if it doesn not line up with Caden's parents wants and needs. They have decided that their child is destined to take over the family farm. Because they have envisioned a life for themselves where their offspring carries on the family legacy, how could a child of theirs possibly want anything different? Or, due to their personal life experiences they have created an environment where there is no encouragement to do anything more than what has already been decided for everyone at least two generatons before them. In this scenario the freedom to decide his fate is being withheld from Caden before he is even conceived and born.

Now for some, this dynamic may fit perfectly. They know what they are going to do when they grow up, they have the stability of not having to explore and discover, their world is stable and predictable just the way they need it to be. For others, this sounds like their worst nightmare come true. Not having choice may feel like prison for them and they rebel. Some may choose farm life in the end but require the ability to make that choice for themselves.

There may come a moment, early one winter morning when Caden is sitting on the edge of his bed, his body is hurting from the hard labor of farming, and he will look down at his rough calloused hands and possibly realize that he absolutely hates farming. He hates the early mornings, the monotony of daily feedings, the predictability of an unchanging daily routine and the sheer lack of excitement in his life.

The key here is choice. Maybe his parents were not given the option to choose so they were unable to pass it down to their child. Maybe they were given the options but decided against leaving where they grew up and decided to stay close to home. There is a lot of self reflection and bravery that goes into wanting something different from what everyone else around you is choosing. In this small farming town, leaving to go away for higher education or to chase a dream would seemingly drain the town of its greatest resource- the next generation. After a couple of generations of farming just becomes what your family automatically does.

If a different choice is made, there may be a similar moment for Caden. Late one evening, sitting on the edge of his bed in his New York apartment, he looks down at an expensive pair of designer shoes and longs for muddy work boots. Maybe he misses the quiet early mornings back on his parents farm and the simplicity of knowing what was ahead of him each day. Where did the idea of being a fashion designer actually come from? Does he even remember the very first magazine he picked up in the grocery checkout line? Did he stare longingly at the glamour depicted on the cover? Or, was it that his mother had aspirations to leave the small farming town after graduating from highschool but got pregnant and was not able to achieve her dream of moving away?

Does he begin to remember his mother staring longingly at the elaborate magazine covers? Was she charging him with carrying the flame of her unachieved dreams? Maybe both mother and child share a love of clothes and mom orders high fashion magazines in secret for the two of them to fantasize over in the Caden's room late at night, after his hard working father has gone to bed. For his father, high fashion is the one good suit he wears to church on Sundays.

In each scenario there comes a definitive moment when Caden realizes that maybe they have been following someone else's dream. He begins to realize that he would rather be a tour guide down in the rain forests of South America. How does he separate himself from the person he has spent so much time becoming? Does he abandon what his parents dreamed of for him? Does he disappear in the middle of the night to live out his own dreams somewhere in the Yucatan? Or, is it more likely that he will decide that it is too late for him to venture out into the world- that he should have done it when he was still young enough to give up everything and everyone he knows for a cockamamie fantasy.

Yes, the crossroads push Caden to make a life altering decision. Should h be true to his own wants and needs or continue living for someone else's idea of who he should be. But more importantly it sparks questions, "What do I want? Am I just repeating my parents' life? Am I living for someone else's dream?"

When going from adolescence to adulthood most of us follow paths that have been laid out for us. We go to school, we go to work, attend church and sporting events. We show up where we said we would and participate according to others needs-we proclaim our affiliations to the people we spend the most time with. "I am a Baptist...my family has always been Baptist. We are also a family of Raiders fans, except for uncle Joe he's a Cheesehead..."

For most people this is the way their lives have or will unfold around them. They seeking the advice of those that they are supposed to trust for guidance and support. The people they go to will most likely give advice that is partial to the narrative that they are currently living. There is stability in following a path mapped out and previously travelled.

There can be less fear, and more certainty when you become a farmer, the same as your father before you. It makes conversations easier over family dinners-there is a shared common language surrounding the life experiences that you share. Ruminating about the traffic or the weather feels real when everyone is ruminating about the same thing. Besides, who else will understand what you are going through? But, inside there is a small voice that wants you to go skydiving on your birthday or to visit a synagogue to exernce the Jewish faith. But you may be detered knowing that your strict Southern Baptist parents may not approve.

For some people these personal "discoveries" happen when they go away to college or move to a different area of the country for a job. The dependable opinions and courses of action no longer fit their lives and they realize there is so much more for them to learn and know than what they have learned in their community or from their family. For others there is a knowing that there is something greater than them out there" and they begin to search for answers. For others there is an awareness that the words, ideas and actions that they call their own are actually a collage of their caretaker's opinions and the opinions of the world around them.

In truth, the ego software is moving right along, doing what it does best- making decisions and trying to march past experiences in the present circumstances. The ego just wants so to knowo which decisions to make and what the proper emotional responses should be. Caden begins to realize that he likes vanilla ice cream and not chocolate like his mother does. He longs to go to Sunday dinners because it's a family tradition, even though his father is emotionally absent and reads paperwork at the table all the way through the meal.

To separate oneself from the ego, or even just entertaining the idea of the ego, requires much from you. Most important is the singular concept of being able to witness ourselves objectively. In order to know which things feel true to who we are in the moment versus what feels like someone else's words and emotions coming from our mouths. To fine tune the ability to be so present with yourself that you are able to see what feels true for you in the moment.

By settling into the body at moments when it feels as if you are not completely aligned with what is happening around, the more subtle energies will let you know if what you are saying and doing is true to how you actually feel and who you are. For example: if you are having a disagreement with your best friend and you say something really hurtful that you may not otherwise have said had you not felt the pressure of anger. First, examine your intention. Was your intention to get your point across or was it to win the argument? Did you have the goal of figuring out what the basis of the disagreement was or were you doing your best to hurt your friend and feel victorious?

By taking a moment to assess how your body feels in the moment you are slowing down to connect to your true self and by proxy are more able to distinguish between your true self and the ego.

The ego wants to win at all costs. The ego does not care who it hurts.

Dealing with Fear

According to Elizabeth Kbler-Rossll, all human emotions stem from fear and love.

As human beings, the simple act of living life is challenging. It seems as if everything in the world is out to kill us in one way or another- it is quite a feat for humans to merely stay alive. When you add the layer of "how we feel" to our need for survival, we humans live a quite complicated existence.

*Love is at the root of all "positive" emotions: happiness, empathy, certainty, honor, belonging, wonder and acceptance.

*Fear is at the root of all negative; emotions: grief, apathy, uncertainty, shame, abandonment, horror and anger.

The collection of these terms and the emotions they describe are not a complete list of the emotions we feel when we experience one of the two root emotions: love or fear. What they do show is how one is connected to safety and certainty while the other is connected to uncertainty and lack.

Because fear can be the strongest of the two emotions, we will first focus on how it may manifest in Caden's life. Fear keeps us from moving forward, taking chances, reaching for goals. It requires that we look for ways to make our lives more stable and certain, that remove the unknown factors that can make life scarier than it has to be. And, some levels of fear push us to function in a way that is not disruptive to our lives or the lives of those we care for.

In Caden's case this initially looks like staying on the farm with his parents. As his father ages, Caden will be there to take over and keep the family business going. This brings certainty to Caden's parents. The land is maintained and turns a profit, there is continued income for the parents to support their retirement, crops and livestock can be very predictable as long as the formula for their nurturing and growth is followed. Besides, if we asked Caden's father he would say that it is what has worked for them and many other families for generations. Caden's father, grandfather and great grandfather have farmed the same land. The honor of having such a stable family is maintained. This equals legacy and support for the relationships formed in the surrounding community. And respect feels good and steady.

Caden needs only to step into his father's shoes to prove that he is capable of preserving the life everyone is accustomed to- this way everyone wins. Caden has a viable economic future, his parents do not have to worry about their child's future and more importantly their own future. They are taken care of and Caen's father can step away from his life's work knowing that he nurtured and left something for his child. Caden's father also gets to feel good about his own life choices because he was able to maintain what was handed to him by his father well enough to pass it down. I also shows that Caden respects his father because he wants to follow in his footsteps.

Caden's choice to stay in his hometown would seem like it is based in love. In accepting the reins of his forefathers dream, he is able to make everyone happy. If he proves that he can keep the legacy moving forward then it seems as if he made the choice grounded in love. This makes it easier for his parents to love him and epress that love openly because it falls in line with their choices. Caden is a good kid! It is the least he can do for the parents that raised him, right? He should want to be like his parents if his parents are everything he admires.

Now if Caden chooses to leave the small town and move to New York, this may seem like a lack of love for his parents and the people he grew up with. By following his own dreams he can be seen as a disappointment to his father or seem as if he is ashamed of his upbringing since he does not wish to pursure farming himself. It may seem as if he is rejecting his father and the family that has loved and nurtured him. It may look disapproving or even disrespectful from the outside, how could Caden go off to New York and not take care of his parents?

For Caden, the fear may be what keeps him in is hometown with his parents and all of the people he has known all of his life. Fear of not knowing anyone in the new city. Fear of people that don't look like him, fear of the large crowds and all of the noises that come with living in such acrowded metropolitan area. It may seem that leaving to pursue an uncertain career is just too much to attempt and he decides to stay home where it feels safe for him.

But what if Caden did decide to choose love? What if he knows that staying in his small town is not loving to who he knows he is and wants to be. Maybe New York is where he wants to be and being a fashion design is his biggest dream. Does he show love to himself over fulfilling the expectations of others.

This is where knowing self comes in and is most important. If Caden is not connected to who he really is, and does not listen to that voice inside his head that pushes him to step outside of their societal norms, then Caden will do what is expected of him and not what speaks to his soul,

Ideally Caen would have parents that would want him to go off into the world and adventure. Maybe they understand that his dream is valid, and they may hold out hope that Caden will come back to settle down and take over the family business knowing that everyone has their own individual dream and the right to explore those dreams.

That isn't what happens in most cases. We bury our own wants and needs beneath fear of making decisions that will ostracized us. We pursue careers, relationships, and life paths according to what will appease others. The fear of being shunned or unloved for the person you truly are or want to be is what keeps most of us from living an authentic life

Learning Self Compassion

For Caden there is a moment that will define the rest of his life. Does he move to New York and pursue being a fashion designer or does he stay in his town and follow in his father's footsteps? There are many questions moving through hiis mind-how will he afford his life in New York? What if he fails and never becomes a success? What if he has to return to his town and his dad with his tail between his legs because he was not talented enough to make a career happen for himself?

Am I good enough? I don't think I have enough talent to make it there. What will my friends think of me?What will my parents say?

The list is long and the questions are pulsing through Caden's mind at a rapid pace, jumnled and twisted with emotions and fear. Caden wonders if his dad will disown him? What if his wanting to be a fashion designer is embarrassing for his father?

Will wanting to move away make everyone he knows stop talking to him and then he will be alone in the world. What will thheey do if he needs more time? Will he be able to borrow money from his parents if he ends up in dire circumstances?

For some the onslaught of unsurety will drive them towards the decision that feels the safest. They will acquiesce to whatever the prevailing opinion is. But maybe for the sake of this example Cadence decides that moving away is the only option because if he stays thheey will descend into a life he does not want and die on the inside.

So Caden announces that he has saved the money he earned from working for his father on the farm and that he is moving to New York to pursue his life's dream. Caden has a bag packed in case thhiseir parents want him out of the house immediately. But Caden's father is more understanding than Caden could have hoped for! And Caden;s mother is excited that at least one of them will be able to pursue their dream.

Caden takes all of their money and moves to New York. He pursues fashion with an even stronger vigor because hei s afraid of letting everyone down. He receives a far better reception than he had hoped for and it is imperative that he make the dream work in order to prove that he is capable of making right choices.

Caden is successful and is now making everyone in his town proud because whenever his is asked about where he comes from it gives him the motivation to work harder. He recognises the people in his town that could have been very judgemental and shunned him anyway.

And then the moment comes when Caden is sitting on the edge of his bed in his New York apartment staring down at his designer shoes. He starts to think about the life he has pursued and how in the beginning it was exciting and rewarding but now it is all too much and he misses home.

Caden begins to think back on how he would longingly peruse fashion magazines with his mother and how much his mother wanted to be the one in New York but never made it. Caden thinks back over the many evenings spent with his mother wishing and dreaming about the life he is presently living.

Because Caden is in a different city and now has access to different cultures and a wide variety of personal healing practices, he has learned to meditate and regularly takes yoga classes. The practices have taught him to pay more attention to the feelings in his body. When he want to discover what feels true for them in hard to decipher situations he sits quitly and checks in with all the parts of his body.

Caden starts to think back on the moments spent with his mother looking at their secret stash of fashion magazines. There is a small pain in his belly, something dull and uneasy that makes the memories not feel as wonderful as they used to feel. By learning his own body and the ways in which he processes his emotions Caden has uncovered that the dream to move to New York may have never been his dream in the first place. He has realized that the dream was his mothers drem, something she had talked about so logingly with Caden that somewhere along the line he absorbed the dream as his own as a way to bring his mother joy.

Caden's immediate reaction is to feel sorry for his mother. Shame and regret descend over them and they begin to feel the blood receeding from his face. He realizes that the ice cold feeling that is taking over his belly is regret. He has spent years cultivating a dream that he is now slowly realizing was not even his in the first place.

Caden begins to notice that when he talks about his love for fashion it iis his mothers words and phrasing that comes out of his mouth. He begins to realize that his mother has been living vicariously through him as far back as he is able to remeber and that fashion design is making him unhappy.

Through therapy and yoga Caden can begin to realize that the fashion industry is not for him any longer and that wishing he were a tour guide in the Yucatan is an okay dream to have. He is free to not follow the rules he grew up with and is able to imagine a life that feels more true to who is becoming

Self Care and Self Love

As Caden unfolds the layers of his life, removing the things that no longer feel true to who he is, he begins to unferstand that there have been many wants plaved on him over the years of his life. He notices that the changes he begins to implement in his life leave him feeling happier and more open. He notices the way he interacts and speaks to people in his daily life and wondrs who he is becoming.

There have and will be moments when he looks around and wonders what affect the decisions he is making will have on his well being. He beins talking to a Belizian woman in one of his yoga classes and discover that her family still lives in the ancestral village. He thoughts about what is possible for him shift and he eventually visits Belize with his friend. He develops a strong relationship with her family and eventually relocates to help her father with his rainforest tour business.

For Caden, there have been many choices along the his path. He chose to pursure what felt true for him, even when he discovered at times that he had been listening to his parnets so closely that he never learned what was true for himself.

When deconstructing the software of the ego, time and care is needed. Human beings are social ceatures and need to interact with those we love and care about. The background software fo the ego can and will seem as if it is the entirety of who yu are.

His experiences seemed total, in that they seemed as if there were no choices other than what somene else wanted for him, when all along Caden only needed to make those choices for himself.

Chapter Five:
Heal Emotional Pain of The Past

Spiritual Healing

Spiritual healing can look like many things. From a visual context it can change our sense of style over time as our values start to become more refined. When people go through an awakening of course they experience a wake up call to what needs to change, but often times it has people undue healthy habits just for the sake of understanding the body's natural process. A person could give up on all hygiene in order to understand what they really smell like. Ridding oneself of perfumes, additives, hair dyes and overly chemical additives in just about everything that's used. A person starts to wonder if there is a healthier option or one they can make on their own. Allowing the natural process of the hair to grow on the body is another popular and visual cue that things are stirring in the mind. Anything from long hair, beards, no shaving of any kind for any gender. Make up and products added to the hair start to transform into their natural versions, possibly giving a person a sense of relief from being bound to that way of hygiene, as there are many.

Another visual representation of what spiritual healing looks like is a persons association to material belongings or "stuff". People who go through Kundalini Awakenings report to have experienced the life of having it all before it being taken away for a more humble experience. You go from having matching furniture on credit, the newest cars, extra non used bedrooms in the house, and regular nights of eating out to something less taxing on the resources and metal space to keep up with it. What it first looks like to other's these days is an extreme case of minimalism where you get rid of everything and only own what you can fit in your backpack and others think maybe something is going on with you and you need someone to talk to. Whatever the assumption the only thing that's happening is a disconnection because they do not have the same realizations as you. They could possibly still be attached to everything they own, unwilling to get rid of any of it, constantly buying new and recycling old as if nothing can be used to its full capacity. It's the potential to not be aware of how the habit of keeping these things no longer provides value and it may be time to assign it to someone who could have it in that way.

As you get closer to your inner self, closer to the awakening of your full capacity items around you start to have a different value– you remember its something you loved as a child, but lost along the way. You start to render the items that you do keep as valuable and contributes to your happiness starts to take on a new look. You take the time to refurbish them, clean them, resole them or give them a new re-purposed function. If you do shop, you shop for the best quality you can afford so it lasts. Loving something that lasts is a wholehearted experience that is getting lost with time due to quality of products lacking due to cost. Utilizing natural products or byproducts of natural resources that already occur such as wearing leather or cleaning with vinegar is what keeps you continually bonded to the practice of knowing what's in a product and how that garment may react with your skin because its allowed to breath and is free of synthetic fiber.

What it can also look like is the "disappearance" of your friend, wondering where they have been, why they have been distant or why they no longer reach out. Bare with people as they too get used to your new situation and try their best to cull all sorts of assumptions about what you're going through and what you possibly need. You don't always need to include others in your business if you don't feel its necessary or supportive, but some people do deserve a fair warning that you may take a hiatus. It may cut out that possible chance of receiving a well check from an officer because your 3rd best friend is starting to worry. It can look like a serious cry for help or the suspicion that you should be put on suicide watch. Its pertinent you communicate to a certain degree of what your adventure might look like– you taking a break to go within to see how you feel about things and what you would like to change. Simple, sweet, and still quite private for those who need that safety.

Spiritual awakening can also look like taking on new passions or reviving something you've pushed aside for far too long. There may be a book or piece of artwork you'd like to start working on or a business venture you had been too afraid to take on because the lack of confidence in ability. It can be the urge to finish that project or to take the initiative to see if there is a higher spot in your career you could go.

It can look like an individual who is in love with life and other people as joy starts to consume your persona and speech. Compassion becomes a mainstay emotion as you begin to forgive and let go of situations that hold you to emotions you no longer wish to feel. It can also look like someone who takes responsibility for the way they feel and is emboldened to express that kindly if necessary— you no longer feel the need to lash out, but you certainly will not be treated in ways you dislike.

It does not look like a walk in the park but it also doesn't look like detriment from your point of view as long as you don't allow it to. We would never want to victimize ourselves because we are having a moment with reality, its much easier to try and move past it understanding that above all there is a reason and some higher purpose that may be greater than you at that moment, but in retrospect you usually always get the answer somewhere down the line— it reveals itself if you are listening when you ask.

Now that you've taken in the knowledge of integrative life practices and an explanation of what they are and how to simply integrate them into your life mens that over time you will start to notice change or the inclination that something needs to change comes into your awareness. These will come in the form of experiences that seem a little too eery, coincidental, or are pure synchronicity. They will also come in the form of realizing there is healing that needs to take place and paying attention to these areas and their meaning through the system of the chakra's and any outside therapies that may have happened or continue to happen on a regular basis.

This chapter is to offer a practical approach to healing and is in no way trying to put fear or expectation upon your experience. These are only scenarios if they possibly arise and not a definitive reality for your life or future. With all that said, what's important to note is a vast array of things will occur and its good to know about some of them before they feel like something detrimental, something you're not equipped to deal with, or that you're at fault for your experience. Sometimes when things start to fall away, the day to day starts to take on a new shape as priorities and the innate need to have ongoing adventures send you in a different direction than the people around you. When you can take full stock of what is ahead of you, the chances of your preparation, how you tend to and care of your personal needs, and your reaction become another part where you get to go with the flow of life, realizing it's a part of the chain– resolution and peace when someone else experiences tumult, absolute bliss, and all out confusion.

The last thing to consider before we start is your ability to share for the extension of healing to not only yourself, but the people that get a chance to resonate with your story and also not feel alone in the process. At first it might just look like an amazing friend who too, is going though some amazing things in their lives, or it could be a trusted therapist or counselor that you've been confiding in for some time. What this gives is yet another example of what happens when people come together for and in rally of healing one another by offering genuine words of encouragement, a nonjudgmental ear, or an inquiry to know more about who you are and what your reality is. While scary, while vulnerable, the most impact and value you have to give is when this experience is shared with others is to offer a dialogue and heathy digestion– full personal understanding.

When you get a chance to know the why's to an experience and feeling that needs to be addressed you understand at a fundamental level what the larger scope of it was and how it helped in the process of you getting here and inquiring about how to have a better life, how to achieve an ultimate state of happiness that feels consistent and safe, and ultimately rise your level of consciousness with the Kundalini. Try your best to take in this process and to understand that life, just like childbirth could not occur without some amount of pain.

Quantum Healing

Quantum Healing is a holistic way of looking at health as it incorporates both body and mind. Postive thoughts and genuine feelings of overall happiness and health will induce healing on a level that the subject is enabling through raising the natural vibrations and frequencies for sporadic healing. This type of healing does not use conventional methods or medications for the subject to heal from their ailments, rather its an induction of healing created by the subject. This is one of may ways a person is able to heal themselves with no adverse effects.

It is said that disease starts in the mind and then starts to permeate the cells and DNA of the body. With positive thoughts and vibrations coming off of you, disease does not have a healthy environment to fester and grow with vigor.

Healing with Yoga

Yoga means to Yog (to bring union) to one's body and mind with the use of specific physical bodily postures called asana. Asanas meet a body where it is and is the place where inflexibility of the body and mind reside. One does not need to be flexible to practice yoga, in fact, you become flexible when you practice yoga. Little by little you are able to stretch and bend beyond the previous days restrictions. It is through the practice of asana that you learn where you are in life, it leads you to discover that the mind is the main place we reside. Asana enlightens you to the idea that the best physical practice one can have is when the mind is free from the nagging thoughts of "I cant, I wish, and I wont", not how far you can go into the posture.

Yoga also includes pranayama which is another meaning for breath work. Breath work is when the inhale and exhale are controlled in a way to achieve a state of equilibrium. It works the cardiorespiratory response that encompasses the full functionality of lungs, the heart, and blood vessels. Pranayama can be done independently or combined with the practice of Yoga and both provide major benefits. Through the diverse study of yogic lineages, you learn each one does it slightly different when combining the breath with movement, and will be discussed in detail further along in this chapter.

When we reach the point of physical practice and conscious participation with life, the mental process around awakening the Kundalini starts to become one of deep understanding. When changes are felt within the body, we soon take notice and want to make sense of what's happening so emotional connection can be finally reached– when head and body connect. The movements of yoga not only give the body more flexibility and stamina, but they help you reach a state of ultimate connection with the self. It is here that you work with the physical aspects of the Kundalini by using asanas (postures) and pranayama (breathing exercises) to awaken the 7 energy centers in the body.

Originally the lineage of yoga was passed down only by word of mouth, from guru to disciple, the practice was protected and only taught to the most devout students. This allowed the influence of the disciple to be that of experiential knowledge from the teacher, and helped deter students from being misinformed and confused about what the path of yoga was to offer them.

Over time the knowledge of these lineages were transcribed through text giving a written record of the long ago practiced revered by many to be the one to get closest to God, the Devine, the Universe. The Upanishads is a text that has 108 teachings, and is one of them most revered to call back upon. Another text that contains value is the Mahabharata as it too has many mentions of the lineage of yoga and its struggles and downfalls in Indian history.

A yogic text that is revered by Hindu's is the Bhagavad Gita, the quintessential yogic scripture maps out the paths of all yoga's, made applicable to everyone in any walk of life. It's a scripture that shows one how to live in the now, and how to have a practical yogic practice. Heavy ideas about what god is, what war means, and the emotional attachment to outcomes are all themes discussed at length.

One last text worth taking a look at is the Yoga Sutras written by Patangali and is said to have been written before the birth of Christ. While only 196 verses, it is the complete path of Raja Yoga– the moral concepts and realization of the self.

There are 5 paths to yoga that provide different ways for the practitioner to obtain a sense of peace, balance and equanimity. Each vein of yoga offers a way to get to the same place but through a different means.

Hatha Yoga
A majority of the yoga's practiced in the west derive from the main branch of Hatha. Hatha meaning *forceful* or *ha(sun) tha (moon)* and gives meaning to how we approach the practice. We force the body through a set of postures that help define an outcome of peace, balance, upright posture, and an overall sense of health well being to prepare the body for meditation. There are many fables to who actually created the practice of yoga, however one story does remain true– the desperation to spread the message of yoga all around the world was palpable. Many of these yogis coming from the east, arrived to western countries around the 60's with their own version of what their Guru taught them. Each unique lineage folds into a diverse array of spin offs that offer deeper benefit of physical fitness and promise of higher states of consciousness. Below are many forms of Hatha

yoga, who they originated with, and how they are commonly practiced.

Karma Yoga:
The Path of Action
This is a path walked when the participant is on the quest to heal and help others in the name of the divine only allowing time for selfless work. With this type of yoga you would volunteer your time to a cause without any compensation, just to serve the good and higher will of the human race. This is a yoga where you have to go out into the world and help make things "right", just, or fair in the best ways you can.

Bhakti Yoga
The Path of Devotion
This yoga has everything to do with full and complete faith. It is when you release all worry and want of a thing and let it go to God, the Devine or the Universe. Through devotion ego is released as self identity no longer holds value and the practitioner is left with a form of self realization.

Jnana Yoga
The Path of Enquiry
This is the ultimate path to knowledge and comes in the form of meditative awareness that leads to inner wisdom– that which is not taught but intrinsically known. Its to transcend the limitations of the mind and intellect to come up with a logical reason to the practitioners experience. While the path is open to everyone who seek it, success of this path can only

be obtained by the few.

Raja Yoga
The Path of Introspection
Raja yoga is choosing the path of introspection as a guide to the ultimate path of knowledge. The most "royal" of the yoga's teaches the student to release the self from the material and to go within, directing the consciousness inward.

Kundalini Yoga is included in the Raja yoga lineage and the name is exactly as it sounds, it is a householders yoga of self knowledge and brought to the West by Yogi Bajan in the 1970's. The chakra's are heavily focused upon as reaching and clearing these energy centers are the main objective. This is a dynamic practice that combines simpler body movements with breath work in order to achieve an ultimate state of balance and restfulness to get into deeper states of meditation. The asanas of this lineage are vastly different than most because while they look simple, they don't feel as such. In this lineage, it is the belief that when the body has worked through its discomforts and emotions it is actually ready for meditation. Each set of asana's are practiced to achieve a particular outcome.

Each class begins with a "tune in" of prayers and protections in Gurumukhi (Sikh language), followed by a set series of postures, breathing exercises and ends with meditation. Each class is 90 minuets long and is vastly different from one day to the next. Your teacher will not do postures with you as it is their responsibility to maintain the energy level of the class to be sure the directives are focused. The preferred style of dress for this yoga is loose fitting white, cotton, clothing that allows the body to move and breathe. The color white is used to purify one's energy field with bright, white, light that magnifies your frequency and expands your aura– it is the "color" or absence of color that gives one openness. This yoga is best suited for those who are on a spiritual quest and enjoy chanting and Kirtan (group singing)

One of the best yoga's to practice in order to awaken the energy centers of the Kundalini, but a class may be hard to find– its not as popular in a studio as the others, but can still be found.

What is interesting is the amount of modern yogic paths that have been invented the last 50 years and continue to grow. Below are a few common practices you may see classes for that have garnered success and a strong following.

Vinyasa Yoga- This lineage was said to be brought to life by a Guru named Krishnamacharya. Vinyasa is a Sanskrit word which means " *to place*" and is a dynamic style of yoga that smoothly connects one posture to the next through the breath. Anytime the breath and movement are combined in series it is called a Vinyasa. The breath is what moves you in and out of transition through a specific style of breath called ujjayi or "ocean breath". This low roar of a breath comes from the diaphragm and expressed through the back of the throat and nose cavity while the mouth is closed. The breath is extremely healing and wonderful to hear as the rhythm of movement and connection to the breath quickly enlivens the spirit. This style of yoga can be done in a vast array of settings, tempos, temperatures, and musical arrangements that fit your personal needs of the day. Bikram or hot yoga is a style that is heats its class up to 105F to help burn the deeper layers of fat and open the bodies vessels, muscles, and tendons so deeper stretches can be had.

Typically a person can experience a "flow" defined class where basic Hatha yoga asana's are combined with movement from one posture to the next. You might hear slow angelic music or something that's fun and lively coming out of these vibrant rooms. Classes are typically 45 to 60 minuets long and can be physically and mentally taxing. This practice will definitely get a person to sweat profusely and challenges muscles you have since forgot even existed. This lineage offers some of the best ways to get back to your regular body movements and works to help you engage the proper muscles. Typically after a few months of practice, you will notice body changes to be remarkable and your range of motion will increase over time.

This is a style for any level of fitness, however starting with a regular Hatha yoga class may be helpful to try before getting to this practice so you are familiar with the types of asana you will put your body through. Usually always practiced in a group setting, everyone will move with each posture together and hold for the same amount of time before moving to the next. You may find a teacher offer physical adjustments to assist proper form, but isn't as common as a regular Hatha class. Your teacher may or may not do postures with you while they try their best to leave themselves open for correction or help needed by students.

Ashtanga Yoga- Again in the 1970's after a few yogis arrived in the west from India, popularity around the study of yoga started to increase which sent hundreds of young enthusiastic yogi's to Mysore, India to study and practice the 8 limbs of yoga under its creator, K. Pattabhi Jois. What makes this lineage so different than the rest is that it teaches one to do practice autonomously. In Mysore, when students would take the arduous journey to arrive at Pattabhi Jois' ashram (hermitage or monastic community), they came to realize they would move together in the same room, but at their own physiological level and capacity. Postures are given one at a time for a student to memorize and perform successfully and witnessed by the teacher until it turns itself into a *series*. When a series is performed in its entirety, they are evaluated and then moved to the next series.

You will find this yoga to resonate more if you are an extremely physical person as this yoga has many positions that are not suited for beginners or those who need therapy work on the body. While this is the perfect practice for an experienced yogi, oftentimes students will find a studio they can attend to keep them accountable to their practice and postures, but also satisfying the feeling of being a part of a group while doing it. Day to day your practice will look the same as far as asana, however you will notice that day to day your practice will look different depending on where you state of mind resides. A class will open and close with a prayer in Sanskrit and the class length is from 75 to 90 minuets.

Yin Yoga- To first understand the roots of this yoga we must understand what Yin and Yang actually mean. Yin is the nonmoving, stead, and the non reactive parts of ourselves, while Yang is the challenging movements toward growth. This is one of the most restorative forms of yoga because it uses slow and long held asana's to help the body stretch the deeper tissues and ligaments of the human body. So while other yoga's focus on the muscle groups to stretch and elongate, Yin primarily focuses on fascia, connective tissues of the joints and bones, so the muscles can relax around them. This lineage was created by Taoist yogi Paul Grilley in the 1970's.

These classes are usually a quiet and oftentimes low lit as a teacher guides the student from one posture to the next. Generally there is no physical contact unless the teacher feels the student would benefit from a modified version of what they were doing.

Usually 45 to 60 minuets long, you stretch the deeper parts of your being– soreness during trial is common. This yoga is best suited for those that need a slow and quiet practice that is low impact. People who are over the age of 60 benefit from this type of yoga the most as it helps maintain problem areas that stiffen with time.

As you experiment with different lineages, you are encouraged to step outside of what has been outlined in this book and explore the many other diverse forms of yoga that exists like, Iyengar Yoga, Areal Yoga, Goat Yoga, Power Yoga, Sivananda Yoga, Restorative Yoga, and prenatal Yoga. You will find as you look further that there are still many more types of yoga forming daily and just how easy it is to find a practice that works right for your body and interest levels.

Now that you have a grasp on some of the practices available to you today, lets take a moment to incorporate normal stretching that you participate in that are yogic in nature as you witness how yoga can effect your state of mind.

In a quiet space, stand up tall with feet shoulder width apart. Roll your shoulders back to loosen any tension as you take some long deep breaths. As you come to a stand still bend your knees slightly as you bring your arms up over your head and stretch them as high as you can. Bring them back to your side. Now inhale and bring the arms over head and exhale as you bring them down to your sides. Good, try that 2 more times as you inhale and sweep the arms over your head and gracefully bring them back to your side as you exhale. As you come to a stand still, close your eyes and take a deep inhale and hold the breath, 3, 2, 1, exhale the breath and stay here. What do you feel at this moment? Relief? Do you feel stable on your feet and strong in your legs? As you open your eyes and come back to where you are, you now come to realize that is the way yoga feels as you release tension and increase relaxation.

Here is another method if your body is in need of new sensations or to release feelings of overwhelm. Laying on your back on a flat surface, allow your body time to relax. Keep a steady and even breath as you close your eyes. Begin to wiggle your toes, now moving to your whole foot and ankles, roll them all around, stretching them to their fullest capacity. Now bring your awareness to your calves and shins, how do they feel? Move your way up your body, wiggle your hips slightly, your waist, belly, chest, arms, hands and fingers. As you give the last few moves bring yourself back to center. Wiggle your neck with the use of your muscles, move your chin, purse your lips, scrunch your cheeks, open and close your eyes, wrinkle your forehead and try to wiggle the rest of your scalp. After you've gotten a chance to move every part of your head, come back to a settle center and inhale deeply, hold the breath, 4, 3, 2, 1 and release your breath. Remain still for 3 minutes before opening your eyes.

This method is probably something you do all the time and is a form of ecstatic dance. Put on your favorite piece of music, the tempo does not matter. Gently allow your body to sway back and forth as the music's momentum grows in your limbs. Let the energy build as you sway. Allow the swaying to become a dance. Be wild and free, don't hold back! Don't be afraid to unleash all of your energy into the movements. Release the tension lurking in the corners of your joints, the strain deep in the muscle. As the music fades, bring your body back to a gentle sway. Bring your arms above your head, inhale... Slowly release your arms down to your sides, exhale.

A lot of what we do in life is yoga, we just don't have words to associate it, we see them as activities that heighten our sense of feeling good. Opening yourself to these simple yet effective methods allows you to see how the feeling of yoga works through your body, the sensations that may wash over you and the variations needed to experience a sense of relief.

Making Yoga simple and a part of your day everyday routine takes a new mind set when it comes to putting our body first. Its not throwing your clothes on, grabbing your gym bag and driving down to the place where you follow your autonomous daily routine. No longer are you mindlessly doing something for the sake of getting there, doing your reps, and finishing. Yoga is moving with yourself to see how you are feeling and where you are at. It's the subtlety of knowing that each day is uniquely different, because you wake up to feel angry for no reason and the next day feel elated because the mind feel a little lighter. No matter what way you wake up or how you determine you feel, you do your yoga, and it is what helps you through not only the bad times, but helps elevate the good times too.

For a beginner it is recommended that you try quite a few lineages before deciding on the one you will start your daily practice with. Take your time, there is no rush and consider doing the practice twice before you decide you don't like it, give up, and move on to the next. Its like food, sometimes you have to eat more than once and in a few different settings before you realize you like it– allow the time for it to grow on you. As you move through the many practices you'd like to try, you are encouraged to keep a few in your arsenal, the reason for this is because it feels better to have something else to fall back on should you get bored or need a shake up from time to time.

Decide which one will be your go to, or if you will choose to change the practice from day to day. Remember, there are no rules, if you decide Kundalini is on Mondays, Ashtanga on Wednesdays, and Yin on Fridays after a long weeks worth of work, then so be it. Just keep in mind that particular results are better experienced when the lineage remains the same for at least 40 days– play with this and see what works for you.

Next you'll need to carve out some time from your day that is feasible to do each and every day when you are ready. Starting out, its best to find a time of day where you have at least 30 minuets of open time on a consecutive, daily basis and choose 3 days out of the week to start your practice and participate for no less than 10 minuets each time. After 2 weeks increase it a day until you've reached the amount of days you'd like to practice, whether 5 to 6 days a week or an everyday commitment. When you've reached your max days, you'll then increase the time of practice until you've reached the time you're lineage will require for a full practice.

Experienced yogi's may decide to shake up what they are currently doing by changing their current perception from just a body practice to encompassing a spiritual one. When someone has a daily practice in which they devote their full and complete energy, where they chant on the divine, and choose to do it every day rain or shine, happy or depressed, is called a spiritual practice and has a name, Sadhana. The practice of Sadhana is never easy, in fact it's the hardest thing you will do for the day, and everything else you will encounter for the day will feel downstream. The time of day is important as well, its important to either practice at Gods hour (3-6am) or the Golden hour (4-6pm) as these are the best energies in the sky and when you can connect with yourself the deepest.

No matter where you are in your journey, you are encouraged to take these tips as a starting point for your evolution. Times and days to practice are only suggested for the highest intended outcome and is not a rule of thumb until the test of time. Its much better to adore a practice that doesn't follow anyone else's rules rather than doing a practice you truly hate because there is too much doctrine. Now is the time to start choosing what you want out of life instead of following something that doesn't feel authentic to you.

Chapter Six:
Healing the Chakras

Symptoms of Chakra healing will be on the account of the body locations and the actions of working with the Chakras as outlined in this book. They are of reality and experience so if it is your reality to have some of these symptoms be sure to take time to rest, always be okay to pull back a little and the smaller steps you take, the less amount and detriment and harm you could inflict on yourself. This is not medical advice, so if things are feeling off because of your changing lifestyle, a previous prognosis, or what really feels like something wrong, please see your medical doctor before moving forward. We can never mask our real symptoms with this knowledge and do nothing constructive about it– we must if we are able and it intuitively feels like a real issue. Its good to listen to your body as much as possible through this process as the removal of toxicity and items that serve no healthy purpose are replaced with the good you are learning to inject, take stock, journal and pay attention to the changes of your rhythms, your breathing, your heartbeat and overall sense of well-being over any amount of time during this process.

The healing symptoms of the **First Chakra** involves the organs connected to the Root of the body as it is in a seated position. This would be the sexual organs and anus– the organs of creation and elimination. With that said, what may occur are things related to this area of the body that may have never occurred before that send a chain reaction to nearby areas as a cry for help to solve the problem. Anything from hemorrhoids, constipation, or pain in the tail bone can be signs this area is experiencing a change. While painful, it usually acts as a physical representation of irritation, inflamation and agitation while internally it's a pain no one can see or feel so its as if you go at it alone.

This could be a time in your life where you question your sexuality or experiment with parts of yourself that have been dormant until embarking on this journey. While some of this may feel extremely uncomfortable to deal with or bring up unexpected memories or reactions in others, you are encouraged to slowly progress, not to fixate on situations that seem confusing– no one else needs or deserves an answer, there is no rush to reach to any point or get to the bottom of it for resolution. There may also be a slim chance you will not deal with it, that you will observe these feelings and your own wonderment about sexuality by giving it honor in your own private way– this is perfectly healthy.

Another experience with this area of the body are the loss of sexual appetite or loss of feeling during masturbation as these areas become less sensitive– your mind starts to focus on things it feels is of greater importance. However this may not come until after a long rapport with other people you have exchanged energy with and are done giving yourself in that way. It may come after a long obsession of sex and masturbation. It may also work the other way around where you might find yourself awakening sexually after a long hiatus and are rediscovering your body. Whatever way you are pulled, you are encouraged to safely explore these areas of your body and possible fantasies that may arise. In the end, what it will always boil down to is being connected to another person or yourself fully as a spiritual person forces those needs and fantasies to reshape themselves as a desire of actualization and real lasting physical connection with a focused energy towards as many as one can handle. Practicing celibacy is a common force and is a surefire way to genuine love and happiness–harnessing and growing your sexual power and health.

Mental connections can revolve around any form of pushing past the mundane and a focus toward an understanding of life that's past the normalcy of day to day routines. This is where a lot get cycled through. Looking around to realize you may have been living in excess or beyond your means is likely and survival starts to kick in– you need new strategies and possibly need to let go of a few things. Mental and physical symptoms can occur simultaneously through any process of working with a Chakra so stay aware of the changes and what doesn't feel like you or what feels like it needs to be changed for the sake of your sanity.

The healing symptoms of the **Second Chakra** involves the organs connected to the reproductive system.

For people with a uterus, where menses and baby growing takes place as well as the surrounding internal organs of the urinary system. This can be removed and still experience sensation as the organs and the space around it has repositioned itself. For people with a penis and sperm producing scrotum, it will also include urinary organs. These organs too can have been removed but still feel the sensations of the area when the energies are being worked with. For trans people, this can really be interchanged so listen to who you are and what your body is telling you. You are encouraged to feel this part out, while the Chakra system has been around for thousands of years, our idea's and values around gender and the body parts associated were not as complex back then as they are now. Feel free to play with this area if you are a person who is exploring their gender or is wanting to connect to the process naturally. There is no right or wrong way, no right or wrong body part to have to make it true– the only truth comes from you.

A physical symptom that may be unnerving is the difficulty to have a painless period if you have a uterus that still has a monthly Moon cycle. It can be increased cramping or the passing of larger things during the moon cycle– the body reacts in this way quite often, by trying to rid itself of old tissues and stored painful memory. When a body carries a baby at any point in life, this chakra is stimulated to awaken automatically, it may not fully, but the opportunity is present. Or for a person with a penis, brief dysfunction can be experienced as well as pain or an unexpected injury. Loss of sensation or libido is a common occurrence and is a symptom of pushing past unhealthy emotional and physical barriers– getting to the higher states of spirituality.

Mental connections can revolve around any form of pushing past old issues and traumas from past lives or in the present lifetime. Issues that arise from childhood are extremely common as well as any parental or familial toxicity that has gone unchecked. Again, because this chakra is ruled by water, emotions are the main focus and achieving emotional maturity can be the highest reward to gain so that advancement can continue. Old conversations that seemingly were put to bed start to reappear as old patters come back to remind you that you still have work to do. This can be some of the deepest mental work because it is the blockages of the 1st and 2nd chakra's that are the hardest to surpass and awaken, but once achieved can be rest assured they will not slip back into the sleep state– where one is asleep to their lives. This is the part of healing that feels terrible to be dealt with, helps us deal with grief and pain through the process of learning how to breathe again while working with the 3rd chakra.

More mental breakthroughs and thoughts that help heal this area of the body are your relationship to children if you have any, want any or never do. It revolves around the relationship to your lineage, ancestry and what legacy you will produce to pass on. Questioning your role in parenting and the desire to be better at it is a common theme.

The healing symptoms of the **Third Chakra** involves the naval and any organs around or behind the naval point. This is the point in our lives where we realize how old or young we fell based on the life force energy or Prana we have in our bodies. Ancient Yogic traditions measure someone's length and worth of life by the quality of the Prana or breath. It is said you are born with a certain amount of Prana and you are to not waste it on activities that take away the health and magnetism that radiates from a person working through the Third chakra. As stated, the Third chakra is the center to which one starts to work with the blossoming of their consciousness, toiling with and clearing, polishing and making space for a new person to emerge. Increased amounts of energy can be felt here, it less sleep than previously required, creativity starts to emerge while self confidence is solidified and boosted.

Physical reactions of healing when working with the Third chakra are first a downgrade of one's immune system as consciousness starts to awaken all the parts of the body that need to be worked with. You may find yourself with a common cold once a month, or drop into a series of issues that manifest as ill health and an important place of focus. This may be a time where you visit hospitals for check ups to investigate phantom pains and ill feelings that you haven't had an answer for. You may find yourself on a medication you didn't know you were going to need and dealing with how that increases or decreases the quality of your life and your immune system in the process. When consciousness awakens so do the physical issues as everyday you may be feeling like you are dealing with yet another issue in your life that has manifested in debilitating back pain or a once a month flu that follows you around.

Symptoms of real stress can appear while healing this part of your life and body, again you are awakening parts of yourself that have been asleep for a long period of time, you are bound to awaken some of these stressors until you realize you have control over your reactivity, and the trickle down of stress starts to lesson as you trust yourself with every progression forward. This is one place where we start to realize that the head and body should be connected and start taking more stock in the physical health we have or lack thereof.

Mental healing will look like a number of questions you've never asked yourself, and you may find yourself willing to act on something you never thought you would, like moving jobs or taking on a new exercise system so you can get your health back. Stressful work out systems or facing the reality of your health situation can also contribute to the physical stress felt, but overtime you will start to build an impeccable response system that is resistant to and has stamina for dealing with stressors.

The healing symptoms of the of the **Fourth Chakra** involves anything to do with the area of the heart and the lungs. Because this place is a sensitive spot due to the emotional nature and comfort with vulnerability that makes this Chakra so crucial. Partly, its full awareness that the heart beats in a continual manner if we are healthy and disease free, for this reason, its important to show up to life and our relationships in the same manner. Experiencing a sense of blockage can occur simply because the heart center is unable to open up and trust others. Fearing that if they expose themselves, it may be used against them in future scenarios and could be a possible experience that happens time and time again pointing you to not close up and mistrust, but to understand that not everyone should be in relationship with you, not everyone can deliver in the ways we desire– and that's okay. This healing has the ability to take you back to areas of your life that need more strength and resource behind them (i.e. home, earning potential, and backup resources). It's a place where we cannot be in true relationship unless we experience it on a deeper level by going at it alone– developing self reliance.

Working with this chakra can physically manifest as a change in body temperature as you open up your blood gets pumping you are using your lungs more, breathing more, doing more, and being more.

It is here you see how much resilience you actually posses as you figure out ways to reshape more of your life. Beauty can never be achieved without some form of pain and sometimes that pain is physical as you move and change the energy—please don't be afraid, what's on the other side is more than you could ever imagine to dream. It is also here where some say palpitations can be felt as the heart catches up to the frequency of the rest of the body, like its shocking itself back into functioning. However, if this is associated with pain, and feels irregular or worrying, please speak to your medical doctor to be safe. This is not a diagnoses for a more serious unchecked condition.

Mentally however is when most of the pain begins as these memories get stored within the body—emotions made physical. Pain due to heartbreak, feelings of complete loss, hardship and memories that were never processed. This is where it gets deep, where we peek at the things we have been holding onto that we are fully conscious of. Feeling unwilling to let them open, leave, release, or be nurtured. When we start our physical practices like Yoga we realize these memories are stored in our tissues as we move and take shape of a particular posture to realize, it hurts, then OMG, Im about to cry, but why and for what? This is where you cry, it is the point you realize crying contains cleansing for these emotions that are being carefully dealt with, its one of the softest ways you can nurture them, give them attention and send them on their way. A wise Yogi once said, when you cry, let the tears fall and don't wipe them away, allow them to cleanse you and your soul.

The healing symptoms of the of the **Fifth Chakra** resemble anything that deals with the areas and organs of the body between the ears and the shoulders. Oftentimes this is the breakthrough area we reach where a discovery is made about our ability to hear outside of normal range or logical explanation. This is the place where we learn that our listening skills are lacking or are on point with collective conversation and presence. Here is when we have realized if we have given our power away and when we feel we need to rediscover our voice. Inner truths come out here and unspoken words become alive and ready to step out to face the music. Your beliefs here can become so ingrained that your comfort with the knowledge and practices you hold, that being right, creating conflict or proving a point doesn't overshadow and dominate the ego.

Physical healing in this area can be earaches, intense non allergenic nasal flare ups, or loss of voice. It is here where long time smokers realize there is something that has changed and if they continue to give their voice away by inhaling smoke, by tamping down their emotions, they will never get the chance to fully live and speak their truth. In time they realize its time to quit or they feel ready or compelled to begin the process of quitting. These areas of the body are going through a readjustment period and its helpful to research natural ways to remedy any pain if felt or to use natural methods to help the ears nose and throat expel toxins and mucous. Again, you know if you are sick or if you should go to the doctor to be sure that you are not, rule out all options so you are safe in this process of awakening, adding anxiety, what ifs and long hours on the internet searching for your symptoms can create a lot of unneeded energy.

Mental healing around these areas can help you deal with how you spend your time and where it gets spent the most. You can feel run down and tired by the mundane practices you've kept up with and now feel emboldened to utilize your time in a new way. You start to express these things out loud more often and people start to get to know the real you. This can feel like exposure, you may not want others to know about your life or your journey, but the idea is to try your best. People, whey seemingly nosey are just curious about the changes in your life. The conversation however will quickly turn from either inquiring minds to confusion and silence because these people are not motivated and geared up by the changes you are experiencing. Or they become more interested or divulge to you their feelings or experiences with the same subjects of likes, dislikes and cosmic connections. You just never know, so choose wisely but don't be afraid to risk, open up and enjoy listening to another experience and perspective on life.

The healing symptoms of the of the **Sixth Chakra** involves the head and the middle of the brow. This area deals with the complexities of a humans inner sight. The eye that is closed to the outside world and focused on the intention, purpose and expansion of the consciousness and self-knowledge. It is here where people decide that their devotional practice needs more intensity, longer times and more study and research to connect. There could be an obsessive process to this where you must consume, see and experience everything you possibly can, where most opportunities seem attainable and where hopes and dreams start to take shape visually. This is a place where you utilize the abilities of your intuition and inner guidance rather than the guru's, books, or online personalities that tout what truly works.

Physical healing that takes place can look like increased headaches, unstoppable mental chatter or a complete sense of relaxation and trust. Visualizations could also be an occurrence as you begin to further promote longer lengths of time in devotion so messages can be easily received. You could find yourself easily distracted or start to feel "off" while in large groups of people.

The mental faculties are seriously challenged with this area, you will be encouraged by your internal free will, to redirect your life so you can remain in states of bliss and peace longer. This is where many start to notice their ability to see the future or intuit what people are going to do before they actually do it. It is where dreams start to take on a new meaning as the faces and activities performed in the dreams start to make sense in a conscious way while awake and point to larger themes and connections in your life. Reshaping the way you think and how you perceive your life will become impossible to ignore as you realize a lot of what you once believed has now been replaced with a higher level of consciousness and self awareness. While in the space of healing the Third Eye you may find yourself unable to connect verbally with people because you feel as if you are on a level at first. People will move slow around you, stare at you when you talk or look confused by the way you move. This doesn't stay for long, but as you move around you will either take a step back to reduce this feeling or move forward with it because you don't mind the extra attention it brings.

The healing symptoms of the of the **Seventh Chakra** involves working with the top of the head and connecting to the higher realms of your subtle body. Attaining this level of awakening opens faculties most people are not able to speak on because they haven't reached it. This is the ultimate state of bliss and what most people try to obtain in order to experience Enlightenment like the Buddha or Jesus. By the time most people get here, they forget the place they came from as they have been reborn and directed to serve life in a different way— not many can choose this path, it usually finds them as they end up in some scenario offering advice to those attached to the material world and no connection with the ethereal.

Physically this can manifest as anything and happen at anytime. Enlightenment is said to bring no more suffering and pain, so it might be safe to assume there may be physical reactions at first and then long moments of no pain. This experience could really be so much more and as time moves forward more and more people become enlightened and share the process of what its like. Personal experience with this holds the torch in authority so choose who you listen to wisely.

Mentally this can look like anything, some might say its crazy, some may say it's a heightened level of consciousness and you should be followed and answer questions to other seekers on how you have obtained and do maintain this level of consciousness.

What's most exciting about the last chakra is not really knowing the full potential of what can happen when you reach the level of no suffering. While life happens, your reaction and perception of if has completely changed that there is not semblance of the person that once was. Just a gentle soul that has the sight beyond sight, the desire to be one with the Devine and the ability to share this gift with the many people wondering how to obtain it.

Those are all some of the most common experiences when working with healing the 7 chakra's and how to accept this energy. It's a level of trust within the self and humanity that you continue to progress to the next stages of awakening. Noticing the subtle non threatening changes that occur is one of the most rewarding take away's– you're fully aware of when things shifted and exactly why they are different. Living in a new way, while exciting can still have drawbacks due to backlash from others that don't understand your vision. The following sections will outline how to best approach the situation when this phase of your life turns up and the best strategies for success and emotional health.

High Vibration Practices

Creating a home that feels free and clear is an art form anyone can learn to practice on their own. Here we will teach you some essential practices that clear stagnant energies from your home, to help compartmentalize certain areas to focus on first and to reduce the anxiety around adapting your physical surroundings to the new state of mind you wish to have. Firstly, you are not required to spend any money for these practices, likely you have some of the things used lying around your home waiting to be used. Some of these methods come from yogic traditions and ones learned through Esoteric practices and can be understood as a "ritual or ceremony" that asks the higher powers that be, for help to cleanse, clear, and purify the area you live in– an open invitation to allow the mind to wander and discover. Visual and energetic freedom of the mind is to exercise its creativity and access to options.

This works with the Kundalini and the 7 chakra's because it allows the energy centers to rotate and evolve through the places and activities you spend the most time. When your vibration is high it means you are an attraction to positive interaction and deflection of ill will. Conversely, if your vibration is low it can be felt as a gnawing negativity constant feelings of lack and discomfort. Anything you can do to increase the energy of your spaces is just one more chance to get to the higher realms of your consciousness and happiness. If you don't do it because its just not something you do, then please open up to the practice of doing it solely to keep your energy centers aligned, your vibrational frequency high and to maintain the opening and release of the Kundalini Shakti within you.

Like stated in your sleeping practices, its imperative that you try your best to rid your space of clutter and unnecessary things that no longer have a sense of purpose or connection any longer. Remove any impediments from entrances or exits that do not allow for a free flow of air to move thought it. Reduce the amount of items sitting around that don't have a proper place, or slowly start to create the space needed for these things to be. Coats hanging off the back of couches or shoes underneath tables only adds to frustration and looks of being unkempt. What's really occurring is the energy of your entire day, or at least when you were out wearing that item is now lying around your house. Whether it be favorable or unsavory energies you experienced with that item, its best to put them in the place of items like this— each area can be focused to a sole purpose or place based on what it was used for. Items that have been taken around town need a proper place and all of the items with that energy need to be grouped together.

Shoes, backpacks, purses and jackets along with keys, sunglasses and masks all need to be kept in areas that are easy to reach, but are understood to be covered in the energies of the places you took them in. While they are not bad energies, they are busy energies and having that business anywhere near an area that needs serenity or connection with others is a recipe for disaster and distraction. Clean clothes need to be away from the dirty ones, do not keep them in the same closet— a bathroom is a better place. Your shoes should be left at the door. Keeping shoes that have walked all around town are essentially covered in dirt, grease, dust or grime. It's a great idea to keep these contaminations off of the floor you'd like to lay flat on, where your kids rest and relax, or the place where you play and wrestle with the dog. These are sacred things you are able to do and keeping this space as clean as possible without shoes is one of the best practices.

Conscious thought about the chemicals you use to clean your home should be considered a bit going forward. Firstly you want to reduce the amount of products that do a specific thing. Bleach is an amazing disinfectant and when mixed with 50% water and a few drops of essential oil, you create a sense of clean and actually clean your space exceptionally well. Vinegar and water is another great solution for cleaning windows and disinfecting surfaces. Running a hand over an area cleaned with this solution is bound to notice its squeaky clean effect. Lastly, there are alternatives to things that clean toilets and showers, one is Borax and the other is Citric Acid. Both found naturally on earth, these items can create the paste like substance and abrasive qualities you may be looking for. There is no need to spend money on the expensive cleaners or "natural" marketed soaps, if you do invest your money on anything, grab another book that has recipes for natural cleaners, you'll save yourself thousands over the long run while reducing your physical contact with things that are not a part of nature and not naturally found.

One important way to soothe your senses and to give yourself permission to relax is by utilizing mood enhancing scents in the form of oils, resins, herbs, candles and incense. All of these can create an ambiance that makes your space smell nice, it gives a burnt offering to your purposes in life and helps clear the space you burn it in depending on the intention put forth.. Lets first focus on the ways you can get particular scents to use, how to use them, and the most affordable options for beginners. It is recommended that you take this as a stepping stone or beginning by continuing to study this vast section of healing and peace. Get creative in the ways you utilize scent to improve the quality of your life and take stalk of your spacial frequencies as you move along. Soon you will be able to tell without a doubt that energy in your house needs refreshment and revitalization and this is one of the quickest ways to get there.

These popular and widely used infusions can be found in just about any store, from drugstores, grocery stores and every big box store chain that sells bedding to clothing. Its not hard to see why its popular and highly supported by main stream stores and online outlets. It adds to the ease of getting to them and ability to replace it as well as keeping the price point low because it is not a hot commodity. These are generally tiny amber colored bottles found in many random sections of stores– be sure to ask if you cannot find it in candle or natural health sections.

The means to which you use these oils varies greatly, but one of the best and economical ways is to by an infuser that you plug in, add water, and put a few drops of oil in. It then works its magic through the vapor and the powerful effects of only needing a few drops to feel the effects of. Which can usually be found in a kit with the oils contained. If not, Amazon, Ebay, or any other big box store online can provide you a vast array of options. The price range gives freedom of choice and has something for someone in any financial level so don't be afraid to pick this option first, if you're on a budget. A few scents below are not only easy to find, but are essential to making a person feel whole and comforted in times of need or people who have a difficult time connecting to their senses. None of the scents below are recommended to consume.

Peppermint Essential Oil- A refreshing scent that helps with nasal and chest congestion comfort. Offers a sensation of tingling in the nose and throat canals. Adds a feeling of cleanliness. Extracted from peppermint leaves.

Lavender Essential Oil- One of the most soothing scents you can utilize for comfort as it has an extreme calming effect. An extraction from the purple Lavender flower. Adds an overall sense of well-being and safety. Great for mental health.

Sweet Orange Essential Oil- A great scent for males in particular because it has the ability to calm and amplify joy due to the increase of calming educing hormones. It can provide anyone with an adds sense of joy or happiness. Extracted from the flower bloom of an orange tree. Great for hormonal health.

Eucalyptus Essential Oil- Used in a lot of medicinal rubs, this scent can be recognized and appreciated as a soother of nasal passages and the feelings of a "heavy chest". Extracted from the Eucalyptus plant. Adds a sense of cleanliness to the home and an awareness of internal health.

Candles
This is another inexpensive way to get a boost, candles are widely available just about anywhere and can range from a plethora of different scents.

You're encouraged to smell a wide range and choose the ones you really connect to. It only takes 1 or 2 to warm and brighten the senses. The wick from a candle can be soothing as you focus on the flame, many visualizations and meditations can add impact with the use of a candle. If you are not able to have a candle for any reason, they do have battery operated candles you can purchase in which you recharge or replace a battery to keep it going. A great option for people with small children or in places that don't encourage candle burning due to fire risk . Choose your options wisely based on your situation, but the choices are aplenty. As always practice safety by never leaving a candle unattended. Below are a few scents that you can count on to be soothing and consistent if chosen.

Sandalwood- A musky, soothing and nostalgic smell that enhances feelings of well-being and relaxation.

Jasmine- Generally a light scent to mimic the actual flower that emits an intoxicating aroma of high and low tones.

Fruit Blends- These can be as fun as you'd like them to be, bringing you a sense of overall joy because they can remind you of times where you felt good.

Cinnamon or Spice- These scents can add a very warm feeling to your home, reminding you of holidays and people you love. Can bring of good feelings of family and fun interactions.

Unscented only Colored- These have the power of still providing many benefits and more of a visual and energetic stance than anything else. Utilize the chakra colors in order to highlight the energies you want to magnify and feel– can also be done with the scented candles and their colors.

Herb or Resin burning/Smudging
This is one of the oldest practices in history from the Greek Mythology periods, Egyptian culture, and even biblical reference has been given to their magnificence by elevating and healing one's life. Its how some connect to god, call on spirits, and simply bless and cleanse their home. Its Important to note that you will need a few items to safely use this as a practice such as a shell or bowl to hold the burning bundle of herbs, a really good lighter and the ability to find the herbs or even dried flowers necessary to perform this cleansing activity. Some great ones to start with outlined below will not only make an inexperienced person seem like a pro, but help you quickly learn and embrace the slow process, a feeling of control, along with comfort over your environment and attitude due to this small practice.

Smudging is the practice of utilizing the smoke from these herbs, resins, or dried flowers to call for specific energies and clearings in every space in your home by dowsing the space with the aromatic smoke rising from its lit cherry. This process is used to clean a whole house, to cleanse ones personal energy and body before a practice, or to offer a specific prayer to someone you love.

Sage (slow growing bush & herb)- Traditional Chinese healers, Ayurvedic physicians, healers of ancient Greece and Rome have all utilized sage as a healing botanical. Not only can this be consumed as a spice for added benefit, when bought in a bundle from a good source, you get the added benefit of exhaling the scent and allowing it to encapsulate the delicate fabrics in your home for a few moments. Usually used in conjunction with a bowl so the ash has a place to go while you either walk around your house to cleanse or you allow it so sit next to you during a meditation or visualization.

Palo Santo (special wood)- This wood is getting increasingly hard to find and those on the market begin to flood the mainstream area's of our lives. When burned it has a wonderful aromatic smoke that emanates from it, usually needing a bowl or special tray to hold it and allow it to burn freely. If you obtain this special wood, take care to where it comes from and its original source, order enough for yourself to reduce your footprint and use wisely so it lasts as long as possible. This can help change the current system beginning to resemble greed. This acts as a barrier for unwanted energies that are of malice or ill intent, increases the energy and cleansing abilities of a space or object.

Frankincense and Myrrh (resin)- An ancient and biblically referenced resin burned to purify and pay homage to Jesus or biblical study. Expensive in nature but goes a long way due to the way its used. The resin comes in the form of a sticky substance that is put into a safe bowl or burner. It is then lit on fire and the resin begins to gently smoke. Musky, nostalgic scent of deep woods and soft flowers. Learning more about this practice can offer some real benefits to those who want to create more ceremony for themselves.

Again, it is recommended that you investigate further with your nasal pallette— essentially, what works for you and your body, allergen levels, and particular likes and dislikes. When you choose scents that are right for you, the only thing to do next is to pick the source you'd like to find it in and the way you'd like to use it and practice with it. There are many more options and ways to indulge the senses of smell. Trying them all is of great benefit as all of them provide a different essence, but all in all this process mimics the utilization and ceremonial properties of the fire element and its intoxicating, cleansing abilities.

When you want to create a ceremony, it's a matter of thinking or saying out loud what you'd like to happen with your full and complete intention behind it. Asking your higher power for guidance and giving thanks to the fire/energy that lights or supports whatever method you are using is essential. No need to worry if it works or not, you will be the judge as you move throughout your days less attached to the outcome, but watching it unfold. The more connected you are to the greater picture and less defined by the personal goal, the easier this energy can work with you. By asking for things personally, you can ask for them on a global scale, in addition to asking for safe passage or communication with the people you love. Recognize this is your power to do, it is not a foreign craft, its ingrained from parts of your ancestry– not of religious or particular practice. This is only to keep you connected to your divine ability to manifest with your words, intentions, and the use of the elements.

Example of a blessing to use
This is a short example of what a blessing, offering, or cleansing ceremony can have. You are greatly encouraged to use your creative skills and personal/global needs to use as your frame of reference. Above all, have fun with this, there is no right or wrong way, only that it comes from your heart.

"Thank you to this day, thank you for this life and thank you for the newness I am shown. I humbly ask for a cleansing of my space and to manifest only what's meant for me."

NOW YOU MAY LIGHT OR TURN ON YOUR MEDIUM and move freely with your day.

Chapter Seven:
Accessing the Higher Self

Meditation

There is an amazing set of scientific research that proves Meditation changes the structure of the brain. The hippocampus, responsible for memory and learning has been monitored to increase in size in people who meditate regularly and have for a few years. Another area, the amygdala responsible for our fight or flight response, in charge of stress, and addiction receptors in the brain actually shrinks when meditation is practiced on a regular basis.

Meditation not only gives you high states of relaxation, but enhances the positive parts of our brain and lessons the negative responses we encounter. In turn, it reduces the experience of depression and anxiety, overtime improving the quality of lives among millions of people. Over 14% of people have tried meditation, right up there with the amount of people who practice yoga, 7% of children have had experience with it, and since 2012 meditation has tripled in the number of practitioners according to Pew Research Centre in 2014.

Meditation has records dating the practice at around 5, 500 years. It is the seated practice of sitting down in a quiet space, bringing focus and awareness to the present moment and witnessing what comes up. With many forms of meditation out in the world, the practice of Mindfulness is one of the most popular. Its been adopted by those who want a deeper spiritual practice and also those who want no secular reference at all, both just wanting a connection to the self that is of non judgment. It is said that when one has let go of all thought, the path to liberation opens to you, like Buddha after his enlightenment.

Humans are reported to have more than 50,000 thoughts a day and spend upwards of 50% of our waking state in thought. What an amazing set of numbers to realize that we are in our minds a majority of the time and letting go of thought isn't as easy as its touted. The idea of meditation isnt to get rid of or have no thought at all, its merely an observation of what's happening inside your head and bringing yourself back to the breath.

The amount of successful people in the world that practice meditation is astounding, from pro athletes to Olympic medalists those who perform physically for sport often take moments to meditate before a game or event to increase states of focus and to reduce the amount of anxiety and nervousness. Even corporations are jumping the band wagon in mindfulness as companies like Starbucks, Google, Apple, and Bank of America. That's not to mention the moguls and billionaires of the world like Russell Simmons and Bill Gates who brag about their extensive, never missed meditation practice. This practice soothes people who make decisions in the world large or small.

As previously mentioned, there are many forms of meditation in the world and in this book we will focus on Mindfulness as it is one of the most widely practiced, removed from secular reference and just about anyone with a brain can try it. Mindfulness is noticing the thoughts that come into our awareness and choosing the way we respond to them– by trying not to respond at all. Inevitably the mind is going to wander, even after years of practice you will find yourself thinking about past ideas and current things that need to be done. Its to teach you not to react to this fact but instead give it attention and then take the control back by re-centering the focus on the breath, how relaxed the chest and face feel, and how connected you are to your body in the moment.

To get a better idea, lets take a moment to practice mindfulness meditation together. Only practice this if you are in a safe environment where you are not driving or needed anywhere that requires your attention.

Please sit in a comfortable seated position with the back straight when you are ready. Take a nice deep inhale and exhale through the mouth. Now bring your hands softly together and rest them at your lap, continue to focus on the breath and notice the ease with which you are breathing. Now bring your focus to relaxing the forehead, removing tension from the brow as your eyelids soften a bit. Inhale deep, exhale completely. Continue putting your awareness to your body as you feel gravity pull you close to earth, allowing you to sink in a little deeper as you feel the heaviness of your body. Sit here for a moment as you notice the ease with which you are breathing. As thoughts come into your awareness, allow them to show where they came from as you quietly observe and allow them to pass as you bring your focus back to the breath. Inhale deeply, exhale completely. As you sit here for a few more seconds allow your shoulders to drop just a little more, releasing thought, bring yourself back to the breath. Inhale deeply and exhale through an open mouth. You may open your eyes when you're ready. How do you feel and what do you notice about the state of your nervous system? Do you feel more calm or more agitated?

One of the largest misconceptions about meditation is that you don't have the time, its not worth it if you cant have a serious, committed, hour long practice everyday. With just a short 5 minuets of sitting on the couch, focused on the breath, you can obtain the benefits of someone who does it for an hour, while the effects may not last as long, you still garner the positive results and with time, favorable effects last longer.

Another misconception is that you aren't supposed to have any thoughts and you're not doing it right if you do. False. To display how hard it is for a human being to control their thoughts, I'd like for you to please close your eyes for a moment and bring your focus to a polka dotted duck, good, now sit here with your focus on the polka dotted duck for the next 30 seconds. Were you able to keep your focus solely on the duck and its spots? Or did your mind wander a few times about why you're thinking about the duck, why the duck is the color that it is, or what you feel like eating next, you've proven to yourself how almost impossible it is to stop thoughts from coming in when you are focused on something intently.

The idea is to understand there is more to it than just thoughts, it's a practice and its something that is exercised daily, not mastered. If it were mastered, would you continue to do it? If all perfection was achieve in life, would you go for anything more?

Centering Your Inner Calm

Meditation, like yoga, is not a one size fits all approach. Just because mindfulness works for some, doesn't mean you'll like or connect to it and stick with it. Before you let it go maybe consider different approaches that help you achieve similar benefits. While you can practice for an hour each day for years on end, maybe that's not what your life is supposed to look like. Considerations for you should be time allotment, guided meditations provided in this book, or your own seated practice and direction feels more suitable. With the advantages of being an all around better person, why wouldn't we want as many people doing this practice as possible? Any heightened states of being will make you want to share it with the world, or hope that the message is spread across the masses and it is. We all benefit from the 5 minute practitioners to the monks who practice all their lives in the mountains of the Himalayas.

You are highly encouraged to follow the meditations provided in this book as a start to your new practice. In the many, you will find a few that resonate deeply and can grow to feel like something you'd like to do daily.

Body Scans

Here is another method if your body is in need of new sensations or to release feelings of overwhelm. Laying on your back on a flat surface, allow your body time to relax. Keep a steady and even breath as you close your eyes. Begin to wiggle your toes, now moving to your whole foot and ankles, roll them all around, stretching them to their fullest capacity. Now bring your awareness to your calves and shins, how do they feel? Move your way up your body, wiggle your hips slightly, your waist, belly, chest, arms, hands and fingers. As you give the last few moves bring yourself back to center. Wiggle your neck with the use of your muscles, move your chin, purse your lips, scrunch your cheeks, open and close your eyes, wrinkle your forehead and try to wiggle the rest of your scalp. After you've gotten a chance to move every part of your head, come back to a settle center and inhale deeply, hold the breath, 4, 3, 2, 1 and release your breath. Remain still for 3 minutes before opening your eyes.

Intuition

Ultimately the way of intuition is to be led by an internal calling. Some recognize this as a bold move to quit their job only to find out that three months after they left, the company went bankrupt or selling a home before the market crash. People can find themselves jumping the gun on situations only to realize it was the best choice they could have made. They listened to their inner guidance regardless of what they thought could happen, feeling the risk and knowing you'll be protected no matter how you land. People that hone in on this sense are able to take extreme risks that others may not and come out on the other end unscathed, however there are cases in which the outcome isn't as positive as everyone would hope. In any case, the freedom to choose, take risk, and look outside yourself for inspiring ways to move in the world is what intuition brings to a persons life.

Chapter Eight:
Empathic & Psychic Abilities

What we will outline are senses that you will come into as you increase your intuitive abilities by listening to yourself, going where you are being led to, and doing your practice so that your mind is free and open to receive any messages you are to receive. In the animal kingdom, these senses are enhanced for them, they are detached from the emotions, comforts and needs that humans have. They so easily tap into these senses and utilize them to increase their survival and quality of life– in turn we are doing the same thing. While animals may not be conscious beings, they are still ones that are able to remain with high tastes of taste, touch, smell, hear, feel, see and know. If they loose sight of any of these things, they risk the chance of disease or death. The increased sense you experience will connect you back with the natural world, the instinctual self.

One of the most important lessons about this phase, is not only realizing that you have these senses and abilities, but that they are innate and God given, meaning you don't have to do anything but nurture your natural abilities and intelligence, not to be above, but to actually experience homeostasis– a place where you are acclimated, self-aware, physically and mentally healthy. Its good to remember that each of us need these parts of ourselves to be in tune with the larger parts of life. While its not particularly "special" it is a blessing to know we are poised to have our senses no matter how involved we get with them. All of these will give new meaning to the phrase "senseless action" because you'll know without a doubt that the reference is about not being aware, not thinking or sensing clearly.

What begins to unfold is a connection you may not be prepared for as new abilities start to occur. Awareness increases in an individual who is working with the energy centers of the body and nurturing the process of awakening the Kundalini, making situations and feelings more apparent, a possible unlikely symptom of self work. We want to be sure you aren't overwhelmed or caught off guard with the different ways life can present while walking along your journey. You may not experience any additional "gifts" that you didn't possess before, they just may be largely heightened or advanced. To know that you possess some of these qualities without realizing it can be eye opening. However what you will come to realize is that these gifts are within us all and are here to guide everyone if they are personally ready to accept the responsibility.

These gifts are usually dulled by lifestyles and constantly being "turned of" and automatic with our process to life. Day in and day out we perform the same activities without much thought as to how they should change. In fact, sometimes the only change we experience is cataclysm, when something goes wrong or needs to be fixed, other than that we get to the bottom of the issue just to go bak to the automatic state of doing the same things out of practice instead of being led by intuition and spontaneous action. This book encourages you to change your routine and tap into these senses as you move about your day, seeing if you can create your own change and spark discovery as you listen to your other senses as guides toward ease and safety.

Vision

This is our sight, quite literally what we see in front of us, although that perception may vary from person to person. It is the ability to see past what the two eyes view and often calls upon the third eye to enhance this feature. It allows one to realize they have the ability to look into the past, present, or future. Having vision can also look like recalling something that feels true and oftentimes ends up being so. People have reported increased awareness around when they see things others cannot and pick up on images that cannot be seen with the naked or untrained eye.

Other examples of this sense being deeply activated are sparks of light or seeing things in your peripheral view. They could be intense, enlightening dreams that predict an event or prompt you to call and ask someone if they are okay because an image of their face graced your minds eye. Also the inclusion of seeing spirits, angels, or the resemblance of people that have passed on, like our beloved family members. Some see auras, shadows, and silhouettes of people they do not recognize.

One way to work with this skill is to begin taking less focus off of particular objects in nature and to use the eyes to scan the whole landscape. This allows you to open your view and allow more to come into sight. This activity is best used while looking out the window and not performing any tasks such as driving. You may not notice anything striking about what you are looking at, but the object is to open your sight to encompass all "points of view" instead of having one focal point.

Being an Empath

The part of us the senses our body and its reaction to what we are experiencing in life. Its here where we realize if something feels good or not and what will prompt us to stay away. We can solely base our decisions on the way we feel and use our gut as the leader to making choices, often thinking its our mental ability that is driving our decision. By now you are starting to realize how each sense is helping the other adjust and calibrate so you are able to freely move through life. When we open up to the Kundalini and all it has to offer, we start to feel more in the body, especially if we are utilizing our yoga practice. You become aware of where the feelings are coming from, what events sparked the feeling and how to adjust yourself to feel better. It's a matter of being in your body and picking up the nuance and subtle feelings in every limb to the tip of the nose. Feeling your way to reasoning and coming to a logical conclusion.

It then develops into feeling energy outside of yourself that may not belong to you. Possessing the ability to go into a room and feel the energy of everyone around you, knowing who to stay away from and wether you should stay or go. You'll begin to detect when you should take care of certain tasks, tracking if there is a pattern, or the ability to sense if the feeling is new.

Psychic Abilities

Psychic abilities are nothing more than a heightened awareness of our senses. However with a psychic you may possess abilities the regular senses may not pick up on. Some people are able to see premonitions with their psychic abilities– seeing an event before its manifested in physical form. You can likely feel or hear things before other's can, or can sense tones that are low frequency and undetectable by others. There is another spin off that includes seeing people from other realms that have passed on, which is called being a Medium. Whatever the capability you find yourself being aware that you have, realize this is a process of awakening to yourself and not an episode of psychosis– do your best to keep this approach logical.

Clairsentience

The word "clair" is from the french word clear and brings the full meaning of the word to be "clear senses". They are our natural gifts and working on the self can help develop a more heightened awareness around what we see and sense. It is the survival instinct that looks for protection by giving a person more awareness, to help a person develop skill around the decisions that are made. The concept is that you are able to make a more informed decision about if you have enough "information" about it. The clairsenses are an intelligent system designed to give extra perceptions of the world, its made up of intricate control centers that give heightened states of intuitive understanding and inner knowledge. This is where psychic ability can be logically understood and where you might be able to deduce the special ways you sense things around you. Hone in on the ones you feel exceptional at until the rest begin to develop. Remember that not all people develop each one to extreme levels, what may occur is more emphasis on one or a few.

The part of us the senses our body and its reaction to what we are experiencing in life. Its here where we realize if something feels good or not and what will prompt us to stay away. We can solely base our decisions on the way we feel and use our gut as the leader to making choices, often thinking its our mental ability that is driving our decision. By now you are starting to realize how each sense is helping the other adjust and calibrate so you are able to freely move through life. When we open up to the Kundalini and all it has to offer, we start to feel more in the body, especially if we are utilizing our yoga practice. You become aware of where the feelings are coming from, what events sparked the feeling and how to adjust yourself to feel better. It's a matter of being in your body and picking up the nuance and subtle feelings in every limb to the tip of the nose. Feeling your way to reasoning and coming to a logical conclusion.

It then develops into feeling energy outside of yourself that may not belong to you. Possessing the ability to go into a room and feel the energy of everyone around you, knowing who to stay away from and wether you should stay or go. You'll begin to detect when you should take care of certain tasks, tracking if there is a pattern, or the ability to sense if the feeling is new. Clairsentience can awaken old feelings, like you are presently in that moment once again or catapult you into future feelings. It purely depends on your personal experience with it as some paths include more extreme realities such as actually feeling entities or spirits– which can feel like a gift for some.

Clairaudience- Hearing
This is what we can directly and indirectly hear. This can range from any of the normal sounds of the day to day like traffic, neighboring pets, and people moving around to very low tones and frequencies that sound like a whisper. It can mean literal voices outside of yourself or more commonly

the voices inside your head– who you think as yourself. Do you listen to yourself when something inside you says to go the other way, visit the store down the road, or hold off on that purchase? This is closely tied to intuition, but could be understood as actually hearing another voice tell you what you should do based on a feeling– following your gut instinct. Clairaudience can be coupled with clairsentience because they can both piggy back off each other by using feeling as the determining factor to "hear" what the right choice is.

The reality however is that hearing encompasses more than just an audible sound, it encompasses a higher frequency, picking up the small nuances of sound waves. This is best described as having an encounter with someone and as soon as you hear their voice you are automatically alert, in tune and engaged. They emit a radio wave that is of a higher vibration and you can intrinsically feel how good it actually is, therefore it makes you feel like you've known the person forever, or they like you, have the ability to discuss subjects that are of high calabur for long periods of time.

Its hearing encouraging words and taking it into the body, resulting in goose bumps, feelings of elation, or feeling overcome with emotion. This also includes the hearing impaired community as they feel and respond to vibrations and sound currents through their body– hearing is not just done with the ears. Hearing is an all encompassing experience– you utilize your other senses to get you to higher frequencies and vibrations. These vibrations not only keep you on higher ground and level mind, but you are more apt to be open to experiences that enrich your life and staying away from ones that don't.

Claircognizance- Knowing

The experience of knowing is a mental, emotional, and physical process that utilizes clairsentience, clairaudience, and clairvoyance to make it come to life. It's the feeling of being absolutely sure about something mentally and willing to move forward. But in fact, its larger than that and encompasses what we've covered in the book up until now, and that is having a trust in the bigger picture. Knowing life has to offer far more than you could possibly conjure for yourself. When you believe in something higher than yourself, and put trust and faith into that process, you find yourself with claircongnizance– to be led by more.

Ultimately this is the way of intuition and being led by an internal calling. Some recognize this as a bold move to quit their job only to find out that three months after they left, the company went bankrupt or selling a home before the market crash. People can find themselves jumping the gun on situations only to realize it was the best choice they could have made. They listened to their inner guidance regardless of what they thought could happen, feeling the risk and knowing you'll be protected no matter how you land. People that hone in on this sense are able to take extreme risks that others may not and come out on the other end unscathed, however there are cases in which the outcome isn't as positive as everyone would hope. In any case, the freedom to choose, take risk, and look outside yourself for inspiring ways to move in the world is what claircognizance brings to a persons life.

The Third Eye

We will get into the depths of the Third Eye and we will discuss the concept of what it is and how it intertwines with normal functions and actual body parts and organs within the body. The Third Eye is not some New Age fad word about being "woke". It directly linked with your intuitive sense of sight. Its how you stay out of danger, avoid pitfalls, and make a left because it seemed safer when in actuality, you should have turned right. The Third Eye is a representation of having the foresight to make decisions that best suit your cosmology.

Your Third Eye is the sight within the dream state that is remembered when we awaken, it's the feeling of tension between the brow when you don't understand, or a tingling sensation when you eat fresh, pure, juices, foods, or smoothie's. It's the reminder to stay aware, observe your surroundings carefully and know when to adapt if necessary. It is a sight between the eyes that we may not normally sense with the two we read with, however there are people who do which is called Clairsentience and a part of the Psychic or Clairsenses people experience as a result to being open to seeing beyond what others term "reality". We will discuss the Clair's more carefully in Chapter 10.

The Pineal Gland operates the glandular system located between the hemispheres of our brain and is responsible for secreting Melatonin. Melatonin is what helps regulate the sleep and wake cycles of our life—our circadian rhythm. Its renowned as being responsible for our extra sensory awareness and what some constitute as ultimate enlightenment. Over time with improper eating and consumption of toxic beverages, age, and disease, calcification begins to take place.

Other traditions that talk about the Awakening of the Kundalini talk about the Pituitary gland being the central location for keeping the bodies balance and rhythm aligned. The Pituitary glad is the gland of all glands and is the central gate keeper for the functionality and performance of the glandular system. Because this gland would control the Pineal, some say this would be the superior gland to assign to the Third Eye, but it is up for debate because each experience is different. How do you know which one is activated if you've never tried it for yourself? And if all of these Yogis and practitioners know the organs, how could one be wrong and the other be correct? The Third Eye allows us the sight to see that it doesn't matter much, what matters is the practice and attainment of reaching awakening or enjoying the activation of the Chakra system.

Both of these areas of the head combined spell a message that's loud and clear—connection to your natural rhythm is essential for getting closer to your purpose in life. You ultimately clarify your vision and it works to keep you on track to continue your daily practices so you obtain your ultimate goals. A vast amount of people have upset sleeping patterns, the muscles are unable to fully relax and the mind races with all the thoughts of lack, responsibilities and endless to-do lists. Poor posture, the wrong pillow, or the wrong temperature in your room can also lead to nights of tossing and turning. This ripples to your circadian rhythm (natural time cycle) aiding in your 3pm crash, midnight social media binges to "get sleepy" or needing the TV on to fall deeply asleep. While we all suffer from these temptations and issues, the good news is there are ways to improve–not to perfect, but to increase energy to continue on, improving day by day, small incremental steps towards happiness. More to come on the subject of sleep in Chapter Four.

These subjects are implemented in a chapter of its own for you to connect to the inner and outer workings of verbiage people use to describe an ultimate state of being by Awakening the Kundalini and Opening the Third Eye.

Why would a Third Eye be closed? It's not necessarily closed and needs to be open but is a metaphorical concept for being unaware of the larger themes of life– what is actually attained is activation. It is when people are unable to see the bigger reasons for the experience they are having and have the inability to see it in another light. When a Third Eye is open/Awakened a person takes direct responsibility for the knowledge the consume, the people they take information from, and the transformation of patterns that no longer bring joy, light, harmony and peace. The closure however is a true concept for what it should actually look like, an eye closed and focused on the inner workings of the subject.

When you open/Awaken your Third Eye, it is because you have unlocked and continue to work with the other energies of your Chakra system. The Third Eye is the Sixth Chakra out of 7, it is the second from the last to attain "enlightenment" or complete and utter bliss. When we work diligently with the areas of our body represented by the Chakra's, we understand how connected we are internally. We can see clearly how our thoughts located in the area of the Third Eye, the center of the eyebrows–the brain– controls how our belly feels (3rd Chakra: Solar Plexus) and how it intertwines with our anxiety and rapid heart beat (4th Chakra: The heart). The things you are learning are real and wholly connected to the cosmos and everything around you.

Now that you understand the importance, you may be harboring many questions as to if you have an open Third Eye, if you can purify your Pineal Gland for better sleep patterns and if you are ready to embark upon the journey then the answer is, YES!

You've chosen this book to dive deeper into yourself, to shift your beliefs, and achieve an overall sense of happiness by participating in ancient practices that help you feel wellness at a deep level. When you open your mind by taking in information led by your intuitive guidance you see so much more value than if you weren't ready. In fact, if you weren't ready, you wouldn't have been searching for a title such as this. Welcome back to the remembering of your inner knowledge.

Below is a list of phrases, questions, concerns and wonderment about life that people just like you ask on a daily basis that are ready to take a leap of faith. Opening your Third Eye and Awakening your Kundalini is a slow and steady approach to increasing your awareness and finding the drive and motivations that make you excited about living each day to the fullest. What's important to note is that you can be at any state of your evolution to delve into the inner workings of the Kundalini and its connection to the higher planes of the instinctual, yet physical parts of the body.

Chapter Nine:
Reiki & Healing Methods

Reiki was created in the 20th century by a man named Dr. Mikao Usui. This pracitce is a Japanese energy healing technique and can be found in many places as a complimentary therapy and alternative approach to feelings of safety and well-being. While there is no science pointing to Reiki curing diseases or illnesses, it's used as a way to manage symptoms of larger issues and helps to improve general feelings of happiness and health.

When a person is in a Reiki session, the person performing the energy work, the practitioner, places their hands either directly on you or just above your body to bring the energies healing work to life. The practitioner is taught to help regulate themselves, and then to help stimulate the healing properties in your own body. A session can be anywhere from 45 minuets up to 90 minuets depending on the practitioner. You will lye down or sit upright in a meditation chair, in order to receive a treatment. It is then the practitioner calls upon their protective practice, focuses on the symbols of the Chakra's and transmutes this energy to the person receiving treatment.

The experience that will come over the body can be explained as "waves" of energy, tingling and feelings of release as you relax and become in more of a sleepy "trance" type state. It will feel easy to breath into the sensations in your body, you may be holding on to a crystal or some type of physical manifestation to keep you grounded, and you will just relax and breathe as the practitioner finishes their session.

Life-Force Energy

Life force energy is the energy that makes up all the cells in your body and makes you who you are. Everything in this world is made of energy and it's a Universal Law followed by many lineages and can be called a few different names, Prana, Qi, and Chi.

It is realized by practitioners who work with energetic forces for healing that life-force energy is a major part of their healing practice. While many doctors and health professionals know the benefits and the science that backs energy work, its rarely spoken about and considered a kind of pseudo science— removing the power of healing from an individual and placing it into the hands of the broken system of health care. We are more than just the physical body having material experiences, we are also spiritual beings having ethereal experiences.

Life-force energy can be transmuted and manipulated which means that blockages you may experience due to disruptions can change. You can turn illness, disease, and depression into opportunities for realization, awakening, and healing.

Balancing Mind, Body & Spirit

Balancing the mind can look like a lot of things, but the easiest way to start the process of getting even and clear with the mind is by giving it space. Space is time away from thought through expansive experience. It doesn't take much to sit in a quiet space and observe the beauty around you. There is no expectation.

Balancing the body could mean incorporating restorative bodily practices like Yoga. It can become a simple part of your day everyday routine and uses your new mind set to putting our body first. Its not throwing your clothes on, grabbing your gym bag and driving down to the place where you follow your autonomous daily routine. No longer are you mindlessly doing something for the sake of getting there, doing your reps, and finishing. Yoga or thoughtful body movement is moving with yourself to see how you are feeling and where you are at. It's the subtlety of knowing that each day is uniquely different, because you wake up to feel angry for no reason and the next day feel elated because the mind feel a little lighter. No matter what way you wake up or how you determine you feel, you do your yoga, and it is what helps you through not only the bad times, but helps elevate the good times too.

For a beginner it is recommended that you try quite a few lineages before deciding on the one you will start your daily practice with. Take your time, there is no rush and consider doing the practice twice before you decide you don't like it, give up, and move on to the next. Its like food, sometimes you have to eat more than once and in a few different settings before you realize you like it– allow the time for it to grow on you. As you move through the many practices you'd like to try, you are encouraged to keep a few in your arsenal, the reason for this is because it feels better to have something else to fall back on should you get bored or need a shake up from time to time.

Next you'll need to carve out some time from your day that is feasible to do each and every day when you are ready. Starting out, its best to find a time of day where you have at least 30 minuets of open time on a consecutive, daily basis and choose 3 days out of the week to start your practice and participate for no less than 10 minuets each time. After 2 weeks increase it a day until you've reached the amount of days you'd like to practice, whether 5 to 6 days a week or an everyday commitment. When you've reached your max days, you'll then increase the time of practice until you've reached the time you're lineage will require for a full practice.

Experienced yogi's may decide to shake up what they are currently doing by changing their current perception from just a body practice to encompassing a spiritual one. When someone has a daily practice in which they devote their full and complete energy, where they chant on the divine, and choose to do it every day rain or shine, happy or depressed, is called a spiritual practice and has a name, Sadhana. The practice of Sadhana is never easy, in fact it's the hardest thing you will do for the day, and everything else you will encounter for the day will feel downstream. The time of day is important as well, its important to either practice at Gods hour (3-6am) or the Golden hour (4-6pm) as these are the best energies in the sky and when you can connect with yourself the deepest.

No matter where you are in your journey, you are encouraged to take these tips as a starting point for your evolution. Times and days to practice are only suggested for the highest intended outcome and is not a rule of thumb until the test of time. Its much better to adore a practice that doesn't follow anyone else's rules rather than doing a practice you truly hate, so listen to your body and mind while discovering what works for you.

Balancing your sense of spirit can be more tricky because balancing something you aren't able to see or sometimes conceptualize is hard. The idea here is that when you focus on balancing the mind and body, spirit comes right along with it. The essence of spirit, oneness, and the feeling of everything is okay comes when you are focused on combining the body and mind.

Chapter Ten:
The Power Of Crystals

Healing Properties

The healing properties of crystals are innumerable because they effect each person in different ways. Some people use them as a part of their spiritual practice, or they pray upon them in order to promote feelings of love, peace, and energetic balance. Crystals can be used directly on the body during healing sessions such as Reiki, or they can be worn as adornments in the form of jewelry to offer the practitioner the benefits as they move throughout their day. Using the crystals outlined below in this chapter will give you a basic framework on how to use them and what specific properties they contain to help you live a better life.

Crystals & The Chakras

Root Chakra- 1st Energetic Center

Work with the Red energetic center by holding, meditating with, visualizing on, or wearing as jewelry that assist with the subtle changes in the Root Chakra:

Hematite-grounding and adds protection for out of body experiences. Dissolves negativity and balances out the Yin energy in the body by introducing more Yang. Enhances willpower and reliability. Can mentally stimulate concentration, memory, and focus. Hematite has the ability to bring your attention to unfulfilled desires that drive daily functions– helps with recognizing and correcting addictions.

Smokey Quartz- energy amplifier, stores, releases and regulates energy while helping to unblock it. Connects the mental dimensions with the physical ones. Exposes blockages, weakness, and flaws as it is all truth enhancing. Aids in shadow work and spiritual integrity. A great stone to meditate with as it raises one's vibration. It helps dissolve contradictions and promotes concentration. Provides protection and connects one with the energies of the Earth.

Bloodstone- known as an audible oracle because it enhances sound, heightens intuition and assists in bringing spirituality into everyday life. Psychologically, Bloodstone can give the courage and teach how to avoid dangerous situations by strategically withdrawing and being flexible when needed. It aids in reducing irritability, aggressiveness and diplomacy towards others.

Black Tourmaline- connects you to the Root chakra, increases physical vitality and disperses tension and stress. Enhances overall states of well-being and heals the effects of psychic attacks. Promotes against electromagnetic smog, ill-wishing and aids

Obsidian- helps raise the Kundalini, increases vitality and protection. Impels you to grow and learn. A stone that forces you to face up to your true self and taking you deep into the subconscious mind. Self control is increased with use. Repels negativity of others and disperses unloving thoughts and actions.

Sacral Chakra- 2nd Energetic Center
Work with the Orange energetic center by holding, meditating with, visualizing on, or wearing as jewelry that assist with the subtle changes in the Sacral Chakra:*Citrine*-activates the Sacral Chakra by stimulating the creative centers of the mind and body. Considered the stone of abundance, it gives you the know how to manifest and attract wealth and prosperity. Enhances concentration and revitalizes the mind. Promotes more joy in life and clears negative and undesirable traits.

Red Jasper- Grounds the energy of the user while rectifying unjust situations. A gentle energy emerges from this stone. Helps provide insight into the most complex situations– clarity can be increased.

Topaz-soothes, heals and stimulates energy in the areas where they are needed most. Helps cut doubt and uncertainty. Inner wisdom is a byproduct as the ques around you confirm what you know and your influence. Great for creative arts.

Blue Jasper- Helps connect you to the spirit world and balances Yin and Yang energies. Stabilizes the aura and provides sustained energy.

Orange Calcite- Helps connect the emotions with intellect and a very active stone by accelerating spiritual growth. Helps to remove negative energies from any space. Helps to alleviate emotional stress and connects you to serenity.

The Navel Chakra- 3rd Energetic Center
Work with the Yellow energetic center by holding, meditating with, visualizing on, or wearing as jewelry that assist with the subtle changes in the Naval Chakra:

Malachite- absorbs negative energies and pollutants such as plutonium and different types of radiation. Activates the chakra's and attunes to the spiritual guidance and vision within a person. Traditionally known to be the stone of transformation as it encourages risk taking and influences adventure.

Golden Beryl- teaches you how to do only that which you need to and is excellent is helping aid a stressful life. It is considered a seer's stone and promotes purity of being and walking on this planet. Opens the Crown and Solar Plexus chakra's.

Smithsonite- helps create a buffer against life's problems. Aids in aligning the chakra's and enhancing one's psychic abilities. It has wonderful uses to strengthen the immune system and is said to help against digestive disorders.

Tigers Eye- stimulates the continual rise of the Kundalini. Helps give guidance on correct use of power and clarity of intentions. Helps to balance the hemispheres of the brain. It has the ability to help people who suffer from addictions they would like to change. Tigers eye helps to heal the reproductive organs and aids spiritual grounding when placed directly on the navel.

Yellow Tourmaline- Enhances the personal power of the individual and opens up the pathways and benefits to glean intellectual pursuits and business affairs. For the use of healing it is said to treat the stomach, liver, spleen and Kidneys.

Heart Chakra- 4th Energetic Center

Work with the Green energetic center by holding, meditating with, visualizing on, or wearing as jewelry that assist with the subtle changes in the Heart Chakra:

Amazonite- The stone has an extremely soothing property calming the brain and the nervous system. It balances the masculine and feminine energies and restores health in many damaged relationship dynamics. Helps to alleviate worry and fear.

Watermelon Tourmaline- the "super activator" of the heart chakra. It helps instill patience, tact and diplomacy. Assists in dissolving any resistance to becoming whole and befits the dynamic of your relationships and helps you find the joy in situations.

Rose Quartz- The stone for unconditional love and infinite peace. It reassures the user by helping aid with the healing of trauma's and psychological difficulties. Helps to transmute all heartache and emotions that no longer serve the individual, creating a harmonious state of balance.

Peridot- Releases old baggage and burdens of guilt and obsessiveness. A powerful cleanser and activator of the Heart and Solar Plexus chakra's. A gem that teaches that holding on to people and material possessions and ideation's of the past are counterproductive. It aids in helping you to look to your own higher energies for guidance.

Rhodonite- This stone is an emotional balancer restoring faith and nurtures love and encourages the brotherhood of humanity. Helps to clear away emotional wounds of the past. Assisting in the forgiveness needed to reconcile after long-term abuse and pain. This stone has the ability to heal abandonment and betrayal.

Throat Chakra- 5th Energetic Center
Work with the Blue energetic center by holding, meditating with, visualizing on, or wearing as jewelry that assist with the subtle changes in the Throat Chakra:

Azurite- Guides in psychic and intuitive development and urges the soul to seek enlightenment. Safe journeys in and out of the body can be used with this stone. Mentally brings about clear understanding and expands the mind. Has the ability to reshape belief systems and search for the deeper truths.

Turquoise- promotes spiritual attunement and enhances communication with the physical and spiritual worlds. A promoter of self-realization, assists in creative problem solving and creative expression. It is a stone that strengthens the fortitude of a person and works well for panic attacks, anxiety, exhaustion, and depression.

Amethyst- boost the production of hormones and attunes the endocrine system and metabolism. Enhances higher states of concentration and Meditation. Promotes love of the divine, encourages selflessness and spiritual wisdom. Improves motivation and keeps you from setting unrealistic goals.

Amber- A fossilized tree resin that has strong connections to the Earth and other higher energies. Helps link the everyday self to the spiritual life. Promotes a positive mental state and helps clear away negative connotations, pain and beliefs. Helps to treat and clear throat problems.

Kunzite- Helps induce a deep meditative state and is a highly spiritual stone. This stone is best to use if a person is having a hard time getting into the meditative state. Helps protect the aura from unwanted energies. Facilitates introspection and the ability to act on constructive criticism.

Third Eye Chakra- 6th Energetic Center

Work with the Indigo energetic center by holding, meditating with, visualizing on, or wearing as jewelry that assist with the subtle changes in the Third Eye Chakra:

Lapis Lazuli- is said to open the Third Eye and helps to balance the throat chakra. Stimulates the chances for enlightenment and aids someone in working with their dream state. Helps to bring in deep inner self-knowledge. Works as a powerful thought amplifier by stimulating the higher faculties of the mind. Encourages taking charge of one's life.

Garnet- cleanses and re-energizes the body and the chakra system. Inspires love and devotion, perfect for Mantra Yoga. It can stimulate past life memory and aid in past life regression work. Activates and amplifies other stones in its proximity.

Purple Fluorite- assists in imparting common sense to psychic communication. Great to use for Meditation. High level psychic protection and heightens intuitive powers and liking to the Universal mind.

Sodalite- helps to unite logic by using your intuition, also aids in expanding spiritual perceptions and bringing the higher mind into the physical realm. This stone can be used to understand the circumstances you find yourself in. It stimulates trust and companionship between members of a group, encouraging interdependence. Helps release core fears, phobias, biases and guilt.

Diamond- clears emotional and mental pain, reducing fear while bringing about new beginnings. Helps to pinpoint anything that is negative and requires transformation. The inner light and soul shines through a person that wears a diamond. It not only works as a creative stone but helps stimulate the imagination and inventiveness of your new projects.

Crown Chakra- 7th Energetic Center
Work with the Purple energetic center by holding, meditating with, visualizing on, or wearing as jewelry that assist with the subtle changes in the Crown Chakra:

Citrine- activates the Crown chakra by opening up the intuition. Considered the stone of abundance, it gives you the know how to manifest and attract wealth and prosperity. Enhances concentration and revitalizes the mind. Promotes more joy in life and clears negative and undesirable traits.

Red Serpentine- a grounding stone that aids in Meditation and spiritual contemplation. Helps to make you feel more in control of your life. Helps to ensure longevity by promoting purification and cleansing. Works to correct emotional imbalances and gaps in consciousness.

Purple Jasper- eliminates contradictions and activates the Crown chakra. Facilitates Shamanic journeys and dream recollection. Aids in quick thinking and promotes organizational abilities. Encourages honesty within yourself and aids in heightening intuitive abilities and sense of direction. Helps align the chakra's.

Lepidolite- clears blockages and brings cosmic awareness. Tunes you into thoughts and feelings from other lives. Enhances standing in your own space and free from the influence of others. Helps to release mental and emotional dependancy on others and ridding oneself from the common complaints of life.

Moldavite- it is said to have extraterrestrial origin, formed when a giant meteorite struck the earth. It is a fusion of crystals over a vast area. Helps take other crystals to their highest vibration. Can aid in putting you in touch with Ascended Masters and cosmic messengers of the past. Helps to accelerate spiritual growth. This stone is said to create properties that can send a person over the edge, use with caution and ask your supplier about the best ways to keep its energy stable.

Vibrations & Frequencies

Vibrations and frequencies of each stone will vary depending on what you are using it for. You will find the more intensely you feel, the stronger the vibration of the stone. A vibration or frequency can be felt as a low hum or energetic spark between the fingertips. Its wise to choose stones that have this feeling to it as it means you have been connected to its properties and can safely use it for healing purposes.

Choosing Your Stone

Choosing your stone is partly used with the method used above, by feeling its frequency and being aware of the vibrations it carries. Choosing a stone isnt so much about choosing the stone, rather it is the process of allowing it choose you. Don't be afraid to pick one up, put it down and come back to it later if its stays in your mind.

Chapter Eleven:
The Law of Attraction

Mood Boards

Mood Boards are a collection of visual representations of what a person idealizes and hopes to achieve in life. They use this collection of photos or phrases to evoke a style, concept or main idea and film makers, directors and creative people have been using these boards to portray a concept for decades. They are used primarily to elicit a particular feel or emotion from the person gazing upon it, thereby giving a person the illusion that it has happened or will happen based on the tangible look and feel of the board and its elements.

When trying to attract the life you want and to be in the vein of understanding what that life truly looks like, this process can really help you identify what you want and keep its manifestations in your periphery. No longer are they primarily for a physical representation, as we have gone away from using printed materials and expanding the mediums we can use to get the point across. This can include making digital designs using videos, meme's and a vast array of ideas that may not have come in a magazine you could cut out. Limiting yourself to the physical representation of a mood board may leave you vulnerable to not finding something you actually want to see because it hasn't been put in print.

Manifesting Your Dreams
Its all fun and games using the law of attraction until one day you wake up and realize you have manifested or "brought to life" the experience you set out to have. Its no surprise that when we bring our energy into focus for a particular outcome, it actually comes to fruition. Its like knowing you want a red Kia Soul and after putting your want and focus into it, you realize that every red colored Kia Soul ever made lives within a 5 mile radius of you. This is the power of manifestation and it works for your dreams too. One rule to manifesting your dreams is knowing what those dreams actually are. Using things like mood boards you get very clear about where you would like to be in life and can start figuring out ways to make it come true. Not much has to be done on your part, just the small actionable steps that come into your awareness as ways to get closer to the goal.

Positive Affirmations
Positive Affirmations are laced throughout this book because they are the one powerful tool you can use without needing to do anything at all, just repeating a phrase and believing it as much as you can. These are phrases you can make up on your own that spell out a particular outcome you want to feel in that moment and there are many others you can purchase or use for free on Google. The power

of positive affirmations can be felt by noticing the sensations in your body after saying them to yourself out loud. You might notice that your body believes what your mind is interpreting too, which means you are on the right track to manifesting exactly what you put your words to.

Using positive affirmations is one of the best things you can do for yourself and you may not be aware already, but you probably use them every day. Below are just a few phrases we use from day to day that can be considered positive affirmations.

7 Universal Laws

The Law of Perpetual Transmutation of Energy
This is a law that represents in plain language, that we have the power within to change the condition and look of our lives. Energy is not a stagnation that sits around waiting or remaining the same. Energy evolves and moves with a person which means that change is a constant. With this law it proves that nothing ever remains the same and no matter how incremental, change can be measured.

A translation of this is someone in their 20's, young and impulsive, this age makes us take risk, separate from our homes, and start the quest for learning who we truly are. However when you reach 30, sure there will be some habits, thought, or beliefs that will have remained the same, but In actuality, there is a vast difference between these two age groups as experience in life changes the perception

180

of what one thinks is true. This represents change.

Law of Correspondence
"As above, so below; as below, so above."–The Kybalion.
What happens above our head in the cosmos, where the planets move in rhythm, also happens down below on our heavenly earth. The movements, gases, flares, temperatures, and climates of what happens above us help direct the energies and experiences on earth– we are part of the cosmos as well. This can also be seen as the outer world and what we experience with our eyes is a reelection of what is happening inside of ourselves. So if you are having a day and you notice either everyone around you is displaying rude attitudes or acts of kindness, it might be assumed that the sum of the experience you are having is your resting state. We use this law to the best of our ability when we can create harmony on the material, mental, and spiritual planes.

Law of Vibration
This law states that everything that remains in our universe contains a vibratory frequency. Whether it is a whole subject, unseen, or in its raw form, it contains a vibration that resonates pure energy or light and makes its own frequency or pattern. This can be experienced by different levels of speech, holding something of spiritual value, or holding a baby. All bring a tone with it and in turn your body responds to its frequency. So if the tone is harsh, you may jump, however if the tone is soft and

pleasing to the ears, you may open up and be ready to hear more. Items with spiritual value can transport you to another time and dimension giving meaning to that very moment in time. Babies bring a sense of innocense to the world, they have qualities that make us care for and look after them, it brings a sense of purpose for some. These are just a few things in this world we have access to where we can avidly see and feel the vibratory frequencies of something outside of ourselves.

Law of Polarity
"Everything is dual; everything has poles; everything has its pair of opposites; like and unlike are the same; opposites are identical in nature, but different in degree; extremes meet; all truths are but half-truths; all paradoxes may be reconciled." — The Kybalion.
Everything in this world has an equal and opposite reaction according to Eienstein and it points to this law of polarity. Polarity can be witnessed through the north and south poles of our earth, th ebbs and flows of our seasonal weather patterns and even Zodiac signs have a polar opposite.

Law of Rhythm
"Everything flows, out and in; everything has its tides; all things rise and fall; the pendulum-swing manifests in everything; the measure of the swing to the right is the measure of the swing to the left; rhythm compensates."--The Kybalion.
This universal laws states that everything contains a pendulum. When the needle or crystal sways to one

side, the opposite to that needs to occur to create a sense of balance.

Law of Cause and Effect
The Law of Cause and Effect states that when there is a cause for something to happen, there is an irrefutable effect. If you push a child on a swing, it will eventually swing back your direction so that you may reach out and push it again. This can also be looked upon as consequences to our actions. Should we lash out or reach out with kindness, both have an effect that will be drastically different between the two.

Law of Gender
Gender is in everything; everything has its Masculine and Feminine Principles; Gender manifests on all planes." — The Kybalion.
This Law is fundamental to creating the next generation as we need both the Feminine and the Masculine to make reproduction occur.

Raising Vibration
What kinds of music do you listen to and how do you raise your own vibration? When you listen to the words of your favorite music, what is the overarching message of what you accumulatively listen to? There is no one way it should be, but take note that if your music revolves around heartbreak, leaving and never coming back, or being cheated on, its an energy that is bound to keep repeating in your life. Words can be spell bounders, in other words when we speak, sing, or intuit words of

intention, we tend to manifest that which we focus upon. Its not that we need to be afraid of everything we say and think, but when we do, we start to see the contributors to our continual experience of disdain or disappointment.

As you will see in Mantra Yoga, the words you chant on intently with conviction, words that you memorize that come from the heart and contain emotion will get you closer to the truth, a realization of God, or the opening of the heart & throat Chakra's. If Mantra can go that far to improve your life and give you a practice of devotion, then cant the music you sing, memorize, and listen to over and over have the same effect?

The idea isn't to revolutionize everything you listen to and force you to listen to types of music you do not connect to, but you are invited to discover the recommended genre's to see if they increase your ability to get deeper in your meditative practice, to write for hours in your Journal, or to make an intentional meal from the heart. Its to remove the thoughts and emotions from the music you're currently relating to and allow your hearing a new experience so that it can help move you toward actions you truly desire.

Professional Interventions

What is a professional intervention? This is a person is usually trained in specific modalities that help people go thorough what you are experiencing with a supportive and graceful approach. These are people that do understand the language in this book and in conjunction with therapy can assist in the full blossom and Awakening of the Kundalini. Below is a short but helpful list of modalities that are safe to step into backed and supported by committees, regulatory societies and stringent codes of ethics.

Reiki Practitioners
This ancient Japanese practice train's individuals in the study of healing with the use of touch. Reiki means spiritual healing life force energy, so in essence, this is a spiritual practice of using lifeforce energy and touch to heal the body's ailments. Highly trained practitioners are able to give a treatment often times not needing to actually touch their clients and healing can be done distantly as people can still feel the benefits. What is fundamentally valuable about this healing is that you don't need to believe in anything in particular, its not a religion or a rigid set of beliefs. It is governed and supportive by a close nit organization and rigorous set of training needed to be called a Reiki Practitioner.

People often report feelings of bliss or complete comfort during a treatment, often feeling lighter. It is a practice in which the patient takes complete control of their physical and spiritual healing by being present for the self when life calls for it. It's a positive way to assist the body through its emotional connections.

Astrologers

Are a part of a larger network of study called Astrology- the study of the planets and their effects on our daily experience- it covers many different linages and approaches to help a person understand their inner workings on a deeper level. A trained, professional Astrologer can look at the day you were born (Birthchart) to see how you are effected by life and how that can shift and align with the current movements in the sky. It can give a person reasons to why they feel the way they do. Sometimes we don't realize how effected we are by the Moon's placement or what makes us tick and why that wont change. It helps to clarify significant areas of our lives and time frames that can give peace of mind and insight into the inner workings of the psyche. It is yet another way you can internally go within to do more self study for self knowledge.

Yoga & Mediation Teachers

Not all people will fall into this category, but some Yoga & Meditation teachers have the insight and training to deeply support someone emotionally while on their journey to physical health and realization. Their knowledge about the body and where emotions get stored is a great way to work with the energy in a safe and supported environment. Some teachers are able to intuitively feel when you need more, they can help you with proper posture and can verbally guide you to better states of understanding. They are fully trained in the understanding of the chakra system as the premise and study of energy in yogic practice.

Sound Healers
These practitioners use the energy of sound to help a person heal the energy centers in their bodies and to help unwind and loosen feelings that have been trapped inside a persons cells. This is the practice of using instruments or the voice to create harmonious tones that allow a person to fully release and relax. This can encompass things like singing bowls, drums, mantra, gongs, chimes and various other instruments that soothe. You can get the benefits of a treatment through a group class, online participation, or a recording while you relax and allow the mind to drift and wander.

Chapter Twelve:
Detox Your Life

Pranayama
Pranayama is the practice of yogic breath or breath-work. It is the controlled process of utilizing the inhale and the exhale to reach a projected state of feeling or consciousness. There are thousands of these breathing exercises and span over many different yogic lineages. The most important part of pranayama is the fact that it cleans your blood as you move oxygen in and out of the lungs. These practices not only calm you and give you a sense of purpose, but you utilize the very simple practice of breathing to cleanse yourself and bring more vitality to your life.

Mindfulness
As previously mentioned, there are many forms of meditation in the world and in this book we will focus on Mindfulness as it is one of the most widely practiced, removed from secular reference and just about anyone with a brain can try it. Mindfulness is noticing the thoughts that come into our awareness and choosing the way we respond to them– by trying not to respond at all. Inevitably the mind is going to wander, even after years of practice you will find yourself thinking about past ideas and current things that need to be done. Its to

teach you not to react to this fact but instead give it attention and then take the control back by re-centering the focus on the breath, how relaxed the chest and face feel, and how connected you are to your body in the moment.

To get a better idea, lets take a moment to practice mindfulness meditation together. Only practice this if you are in a safe environment where you are not driving or needed anywhere that requires your attention. One of the largest misconceptions about mindfulness is that you don't have the time, its not worth it if you cant have a serious, committed, hour long practice everyday. With just a short 5 minuets of sitting on the couch, focused on the breath, you can obtain the benefits of someone who does it for an hour, while the effects may not last as long, you still garner the positive results and with time, favorable effects last longer.

The idea is to understand there is more to it than just thoughts, it's a practice and its something that is exercised daily, not mastered. If it were mastered, would you continue to do it? If all perfection was achieve in life, would you go for anything more?

Cleanse Your Body

What you put in your body is just as valuable as what you don't put in your body and in terms of fasting, you might consider this a part of your regimen to stay healthy. Fasting is not for everyone, so please consult your doctor before taking on a rigorous restrictions such as abstaining from solids and only consuming fluids. Fasting can be considered a daily practice and is as simple as spreading out your meals so that the bulk of you not eating is when you are resting. For example, if you stop eating 3 to 4 hours before you go to bed, you will give your body time to process and slow down before you rest. You'll now add your sleep which should healthfully be between 6 and 8 hours each night. You'll then add the hours after you wake before you break your fast. If your sum total adds up to more than 11 hours of not eating, you are on the right track to supreme digestion, a daily practice of limiting intake past physical exertion, and a sense of internal wellness within days of implementation.

When you clean up your diet, over time you start to sense more about your surroundings, the types of places you will eat at and how often you cook at home. It will become more important to you to gain control over ingredients, quality and time. With this, conscious eating begins and you ultimately fine tune your intuitive food selection and know when to allow them to choose you.

Beginners Mind

Now that you have a grasp on some of the practices available to you today, lets take a moment to incorporate normal stretching that you participate in that are yogic in nature as you witness how yoga can effect your state of mind.

In a quiet space, stand up tall with feet shoulder width apart. Roll your shoulders back to loosen any tension as you take some long deep breaths. As you come to a stand still bend your knees slightly as you bring your arms up over your head and stretch them as high as you can. Bring them back to your side. Now inhale and bring the arms over head and exhale as you bring them down to your sides. Good, try that 2 more times as you inhale and sweep the arms over your head and gracefully bring them back to your side as you exhale. As you come to a stand still, close your eyes and take a deep inhale and hold the breath, 3, 2, 1, exhale the breath and stay here. What do you feel at this moment? Relief? Do you feel stable on your feet and strong in your legs? As you open your eyes and come back to where you are, you now come to realize that is the way yoga feels as you release tension and increase relaxation.

Here is another method if your body is in need of new sensations or to release feelings of overwhelm. Laying on your back on a flat surface, allow your body time to relax. Keep a steady and even breath as you close your eyes. Begin to wiggle your toes, now moving to your whole foot and ankles, roll them all around, stretching them to their fullest capacity. Now bring your awareness to your calves and shins, how do they feel? Move your way up your body, wiggle your hips slightly, your waist, belly, chest, arms, hands and fingers. As you give the last few moves bring yourself back to center. Wiggle your neck with the use of your muscles, move your chin, purse your lips, scrunch your cheeks, open and close your eyes, wrinkle your forehead and try to wiggle the rest of your scalp. After you've gotten a chance to move every part of your head, come back to a settle center and inhale deeply, hold the breath, 4, 3, 2, 1 and release your breath. Remain still for 3 minutes before opening your eyes.

This method is probably something you do all the time and is a form of ecstatic dance. Put on your favorite piece of music, the tempo does not matter. Gently allow your body to sway back and forth as the music's momentum grows in your limbs. Let the energy build as you sway. Allow the swaying to become a dance. Be wild and free, don't hold back! Don't be afraid to unleash all of your energy into the movements. Release the tension lurking in the corners of your joints, the strain deep in the muscle. As the music fades, bring your body back to a gentle sway. Bring your arms above your head, inhale... Slowly release your arms down to your sides, exhale.

A lot of what we do in life is yoga, we just don't have words to associate it, we see them as activities that heighten our sense of feeling good. Opening yourself to these simple yet effective methods allows you to see how the feeling of yoga works through your body, the sensations that may wash over you and the variations needed to experience a sense of relief.

Beginner Inquiries to Enlightenment

I want to know more about practices I connect to.

Do I have the authority to explore the Third Eye and the Kundalini on my own?

I don't feel scared by what could happen, I am excited by the endless possibility.

I am looking for more out of life.

I am ready for life's new possibilities.

I am a Yoga teacher expanding my personal practice.

I work really hard and need something to relax me.

I am unemployed and looking to expand my mind while I discover what my next path is.

I want to start a business, but I feel unconnected to what it should be centered around.

I am an Entrepreneur and looking to add value to my daily life.

I employ a large number of people with differing beliefs who are young and seekers of knowledge.

I want to connect with fun loving people who have diverse beliefs.

I am looking to increase my arsenal of tools.

I now work from home and desire peace back in my home.

People tell me I am "connected", but I am not sure how.

I want to learn how to live a better life on my own.

I am open to any and all practices of the world as long as they have moral value and spirit.

I enjoy topics on metaphysics.

I practice Yoga and want to learn about the deeper concepts of why I do it.

I enjoy self improvement, but I am looking for

something deeper.

I am coming out of a state of depression and looking for hope.

I am a beginner and I just want to learn the concepts.

I am a novice and I'd like another point of view.

The worlds disasters has me wondering if there is anything more.

I am blessed to be alive from the worlds Pandemic and desire devotion to my new lease on life.

I have survived traumatic events in my life and am ready to safely move on.

I see a therapist or counselor and they have encouraged me to explore self study.

I am a therapist and want to understand the people who speak about this in my presence.

I am a counselor and I want to better know the person I am helping who does these practices.

I am a forever student and desire to learn more.

How do I take my power back?

How do I become a medicine person?

I want to help people in the world, but I don't know what it should be.

How do I increase my intuitive abilities?

How do I get my feet wet with Meditation?

I'm not flexible, so I don't do Yoga.

I want to heal from a bad relationship.

I want to know more about the Chakra system.

People always talk about Meditating, but I don't like it.

Meditation doesn't work for me.

Im ready to improve my relationships.

How do I improve my mental state?

Do I have special abilities I am not aware of?

I am doing all the things but nothing seems to be working.

I need help.

There is something missing from my daily practice, but I don't know what it is.

Im tired of hearing this New Age lingo, what is it exactly?

I am a private person and I don't want to take a class to learn the basics.

I am a self starter and need something with substance.

How can I interlink all my practices?

What is the purpose of my life?

I want to study something with meaning.

Should I have a bigger impact on the world?

I am sick of this (fill in the blank) happening to me, how do I detach from it?

I need something more to connect to.

I need more spirituality in my life.

Do I have to choose just one practice or can I try them all?

I love Astrology and Tarot and want to know more.

I approach life with a holistic point of view.

I have the power to change my life and my circumstances.

I see colors, shapes and visions when I close my eyes in Meditation.

I enjoy contemplation.

I go inward.

I want to escape.

I feel helpless at the moment, how do I move forward?

My social media feeds wont stop recommending this stuff to me.

All of my quirky but interesting friends are into this stuff, what's the hype?

Is this some New Age fad that will pass with time?

The list of questions can proceed for many pages, the point is to prove that you can be in any stage of life, age, or experience to be ready for this information and eye opening journey. This Chapter we have covered the importance of the Third Eye, the Pineal & Pituitary Glands, and how to know if you are in the right mental space to do this work. In the next chapter we will dive deeper into the main essence of the Kundalini and the larger purpose and inner workings of its Awakening process.

Chapter Thirteen:
Finding Your Spiritual Path

Spirit Guides & Angels

In some religions Spirit Guides seem to execute the same role as Angles. An anointed being that exists somewhere between the physical and ethereal plane. In Western Spiritualism their classifications means that they are our "personal" angels, here to help guide us through the challenges of human life.

Spirit Guides are otherworldly entities that hover close to the human side remaining unseen and able to help guide humans through their lives by steering us away from harm, directing us to safety and helping us make decisions that benefit us not harm us. Sounds a lot like Angels, right?

The word angel comes from the Old English word engel with a hard g or the french word engele, both words stemming from Latin. In traditional Abrahamic religions, angels are benevolent servants of God that have been assigned to protect, guide and be liaisons between the Almighty and humans. These celestial beings have God-like power in that they are everywhere at all times and available to us at all times.

In the Christian bible there are seven all powerful major Angels- called Archangels. Mentioned in the book of Enoch, book 20, they are Michael, Raphael, Gabriel, Uriel, Raguel and Ramiel. These Archangels possess infinite powers, are omnipotent, and have the ability to be destructive. They are among the oldest angels in the bible, and the most powerful.

These angels are somewhat like deities, able to perform miracles and offer protection to those that call on them while carrying out the will of God, their powers being an extension of God's powers and therefore these Archangels can be considered the right hands of God.

In Easter religions these same roles are carried by avatars, Bodhisattvas and other creatures that carry out the will of the most powerful. They offer protection to the faithful, showing up in times of need, most times just in the nick of time. They also proceed humans on their path removing obstacles and ne'er do wells from the path of those that are seeking God or doing God's bidding.

In Western Spirituality, Spirit Guides may be described as more up close and personal. These are our personal Angels. They are in direct communication with us, we talk to them and they talk back. We hear them in our heads, their voices sound similar to ours and for some this may seem as if they are imagined but in reality Spirit Guides are the louder more prominent voice of our intuition.

We can call upon our spirit guides for things as small and or large as making a choice about the safest direction to go or where we should search for lost items. People with psychic and medium abilities reach out to these guides for answers and direction. They allow the receiver to "hear or see" the answers to what they are asking, and depending on the faith of the receiver can view this ability in a negative as well as positive light.

We all have our own Spirit Guides, regardless of if we know they are there or not. In Western Spirituality Spirit Guides are seen as positive and reinforce our connection to The Almighty. They are a way to have greater and more personal connection to the Divine because at the end of the day,, like angels they are a direct connection to the network of the Universe.

For those that believe in Spirit Guides and work to strengthen the connection between them and the ethereal, there is a personal comfort in having a part of God so close that you can talk to them at any time about anything.

Because archangels are so powerful, they are seen as entities that are as large as God. Archangels are available to everyone, they have been written about for thousands of years. But because they are so large and powerful they can feel distant from the practitioner- something like Saints that have done otherworldly acts. Prayers and requests can seem too insignificant to ask an entity so powerful. They are prescribed and come as part of religion. Spirit guides are personal to you.

Some spirit guides live on the cosmic plane and exist as pure energy or light. Some are deceased people that have paid their karmic debt, advancing past the need to reincarnate again. They now exist to help others follow their intuition and accomplish the same.

Shamans

Shamans are medicine people who assist people with reaching a breakthrough by creating ritual, ceremony and journeying. They are people who are considered to have access to the spirit realms of duality– good and evil. They are able to reach these realms through a trance state that also puts the subjects in a trance with the outcome of hopeful change.

The medicines usually vary from person to person because of the location of the shaman and the type of plant medicines they work with. Hallucinogens are generally used for people to come out of their current consciousness and visit a version that haven not yet experienced. People who have visited and participated in a shamans ceremony testify that they have been healed or have had the chance to actualize or realize themselves.

Enlightenment

Enlightenment has been described as a person reaching ultimate bliss, removing oneself from ego and having no attachments to the material world. But really, that's simply not true in our day and age. For us enlightenment looks like waking up to your life, being spiritually centered, having a heart of compassion and giving all while you wash your laundry and walk your dog. There is still money to be made and people to love when you have reached enlightenment, nothing about life changes, only that you don't react as harshly to life's curves.

Turning Inward

Turning inward is a lesson in self reflection and looking at yourself to see if improvments need to be made. For some people this process is all they know, looking within to ask "does this feel right to me?" The importance of being able to turn inward is knowing when you must take a look at yourself. Instead of looking outside of yourself for external answers and validation, the inward approach gives you the inner authority to decide. When you come from this place, you'll notice how much more aligned your life is and how events show up in your life to suprise you and make you feel loved and alive.

Turning inward can be any form of meditation, seated practice, walks in nature, staring out a window, Journaling, asking yourself questions and answering them in your head and the list goes on. There are many ways you can give yourself room to contemplate, its just a matter of finding what works best for you. Methods to use that make the best of your inward experience would be to write down your experiences and look back on them often so you are able to see the progression of your thought process and connection to self.

Rebirth

Rebirth is a process by which a person goes through a cataclysmic and transforming experience that has forever changed them. This is usually described by many as the "dark night of the soul" and can represent periods of our lives where we rewrite our realities and arrive to a different place in our lives.

Usually when we hear about Rebirth, we hear it in a religious context as in the story of Jesus. It was said he died and then rose again through rebirth a few days later. Could this be a metaphor for how our experience feels in the real world? Have you ever been down for a few days in a state of depression, working through extreame difficulty or trauma and then all the sudden have a breakthrough? This is what it can often look and sound like when a person is going through the re-birthing process of life. Make no mistake that this is not an occurrence that happens just once in our lives, if we are lucky, we will get the change to understand more about our life experience and go deeper with what we know about life.

Yogi's also take this notion to be of a literal sense, but they mention that a state of consciousness is reached that wasn't their before. The understanding in life, the compassion and love that has grown and the ability to look beyond the person needs and wants in life is where consciousness or rebirth starts to manifest. Awakening the Kundalini though the healing and awakening of the chakra's is one yogic philosophy surrounding the subject of rebirth. With the teachings in this book you have the ability to work through and cultivate a rebirth or awakening for yourself, its just a matter of devotion and regular practice.

Importance of Support

What many people may not realize as previously stated, this journey is not to be taken alone. While some people in life end up going this route, its not a route for everyone because we all have a different life experience and perspective we are working with. It's not okay to assume that everyone can get from A to B in the same fashion, hence why we have so many Religions in the world–there is no one way to get the Devine.

Participating in a community brings added understanding one may not have while going along on the journey with no one to connect with. Its being able to listen to another persons reality of what they are experiencing when trying to awaken the Kundalini and bringing in some sort of normalcy around talking about spiritual advancement in our advancing technological age. It is recommended to search for closed and private communities that are free on the platforms you already participate on. If you do not participate in social media groups, Facebook is established enough to help you find a spot to enjoy, while Youtube provides a vast amount of community members with a story to share and a lesson that has been learned. There are numerous forums about the subject of spiritual awakening and the positive effects of stimulating the Kundalini to awaken. Resonance with other people going through radical change such as yourself will allow you the freedom to feel more at peace and a sense of acceptance with what you are embarking upon.

Its also important to stress the need for a physical community of people if it is within your means, location, and comfort level. The reason is you always have a back up of support should the internet not be able to deliver what you need. We all know it can be a place where we are left to be vulnerable, some people feel okay with this exposure and others feel too sensitive to let these things go to the eyes of the untrusted. This is why its important to find groups that are practicing these techniques and to meet in public places where you can practice together and safely interact with one another. It may have to be a retreat, or finding a Facebook group that meets in the park once a month or a book club that conjures at a coffee shop a few towns or even the next city over.

While you may live rurally or don't have the means of your own transportation, it is recommended you plan for times out when you can have these experiences. They don't need to occur all the time, but they do need to be a part of you to enhance your experience of life.

Conclusion

As you wind down to the last few objectives of this book, I hope you have come to realize just how special this journey is not only for your happiness and well being, but for the collective and our ability to attain the same heights as you– if one person can do it, the possibility is open for everyone to walk this way of life.

So often in life we are probed to make changes in our lives without the support to back it up. Far too often we are left without directives on how to navigate life's tricky lessons and road blocks or to even be received in a nurturing way, considering all avenues to continue arduously on target. Here we hope to insert a little TLC and remind you how much your health and well being means so this process is successful– your progression is our progression.

Becoming a student of life is a great way to stay on top of the latest research on these topics and for you to analyze and draw conclusions about your own experience as you do more research by reading books, watching documentaries, and take measures to be a part of groups who also participate and walk this life.

There are many different roads you can find yourself on after going through the concepts in this book. You can put it down, walk away, and never think about it's contents again, which doesn't seem likely, or you can take what you've learned and apply as much of it as feels good to you. Or you can also get very deeply spiritual as you see the connections and realize there is more to life you'd like to play with.

Firstly, remove all expectations of perfection and what it looks like to walk on this path– remember that we all look different while doing it. We see a lot of images these days with social media and the ideas of what spiritual looks like is definitely not it. The longer you're in the game, the easier it will be to spot these images for any true authenticity, through your own experience you'll realize how hard it is to actually look like the images you see. Its not fancy clothes, vast amounts of gemstones, or white clothes. Its your own raw process of it all and stylistically its all your own.

Secondly, remain open about the journey and what you find yourself faced with. When life is approached from a standpoint that "everything happens for a reason, I just don't see it yet", then you might find yourself at ease more often than not when things occur that you didn't anticipate.

Lastly, you should be extremely proud that you desire and are trying to attempt to expand your consciousness through awakening the Kundalini and opening the third eye. Following the practices outlined not only gives you a leg up by knowing parts of the process to expect, but gives you the ultimate freedom to do with it what you want and create routines that fit who you are and how you live your life day to day.

Life will only get more expansive from here, may you be safe on your journey, may you be loved completely, and may you find what you seek.

Guided Meditations and Affirmations

MEDITATION FOR PROTECTION

begin with this meditation anytime you are working with heavy energy or feel like you need something before you start your day

Please close your eyes and take a few deep breaths while you visualize a lighthouse at the shore of a rocky ocean coast. As you hear the waves crash you look up to watch the light go around the top of the lighthouse, over and over its mesmerizing, and soon you find yourself hypnotized by the circular movement– light shining in every direction. As this light goes round and round repeat to yourself " I am protected, I am light, I am love", " I am protected, I am light, I am love"," I am protected, I am light, I am love". Redirect your concentration from the light as you close your eyes. Take a deep breath in, hold for 5 counts and exhale. Again. Take a deep breath in and imagine a safe home and safe travel, hold for 5 counts and exhale. One last time, take a deep breath in and recall why you have a strong and safe foundation, hold for 5 counts and exhale slowly while you sit relaxed, unfazed, refreshed and protected.

MEDITATION ON THE FIRST CHAKRA:

In a comfortable seated position, straighten your back by arching it slightly and lifting your chest high, roll your neck to get some flexibility in the shoulders. Be sure your sit bones are firmly planted, don't be afraid to move and lift the flesh around your thighs to make sure you feel firmly planted. Place the backs of your hands on the tops of your thighs, palms to the sky as you put your hands in Gian Mudra. First finger and thumb will touch at the tips making a zero while the other fingers stick out straight in front of them, stacked together. Take three long deep breaths, each one bringing you deeper into your body, each one relieving tension in the chest and back. Check your posture again, back straight, chest up, and chin slightly tucked in.

Bring your awareness to the area that is making contact with the ground, this is the root of your life, the place where you create and join with another and the place where you eliminate. As you bring your awareness to this area, notice if you feel any sensations in this area, pulsing, tingling, or if there is no sensation at all. Continue to relax as you visualize the color red. If anything comes to your mind, observe it, but do not allow it to change your emotions just yet, continue to breathe and visualize the color red. May the lessons of this journey come forth in love and in time. Inhale long deep breaths and exhale the air completely from your lungs.

MEDITATION FOR THE SECOND CHAKRA:

In a comfortable seated position, straighten your back by arching it slightly and lifting your chest high, roll your neck to get some flexibility in the shoulders. Be sure your sit bones are firmly planted, don't be afraid to move and lift the flesh around your thighs to make sure you feel firmly planted. Place the backs of your hands on the tops of your thighs, palms to the sky as you put your hands in Gian Mudra. First finger and thumb will touch at the tips making a zero while the other fingers stick out straight in front of them, stacked together. Take three long deep breaths, each one bringing you deeper into your body, each one relieving tension in the chest and back. Check your posture again, back straight, chest up, and chin slightly tucked in.

Bring your awareness to the area of your body that contains your reproductive organs– the base of the spine and all organs around it. Allow your mind to focus on this area while visualizing the color orange. Allow anything to come up for you that may need your mental attention, if you find yourself in an emotional place, let it out. Notice if this area has any sensations that you can feel and observe if they are linked with a specific state or emotion. May the lessons of this journey come forth in curiosity and be free from judgment. Inhale long deep breaths and exhale the air completely from your lungs. When complete, inhale deeply and exhale with an open mouth three times. You may sit here as long as you need, you should be proud of yourself.

MEDITATION ON THE SELF

It is a warm spring day, white fluffy clouds are passing by as you feel a cool and gentle breeze graze your cheek, you are reminded of something so sweet, what is it? As you take a seat on the grass, you notice how cool and damp it feels and you lean back to prop your hands behind your head and cross your legs. Smile and look up towards the sky, what do you see? As you lay upon the grass sink your shoulders and back into the cold ground making yourself more comfortable. Take a deep breath in and slowly remove your inner self away from your body as you slowly exhale, floating above yourself. Do you see your posture and what you look like? As yourself, ask...who am I?: I SEE WHO I AM

MEDITATION FOR FRIENDS

In this moment your life is together, your affairs are taken care of, and you are able to rest comfortably– there is nothing you need to do at this moment. As you imagine how easy it is to sit here, imagine yourself leaving to go somewhere like the grocery store and driving to your job. Now that you have some time, you can get to know that person who is always so nice to you, but you never have time to get to know because you're always in a rush. What was their name again? If you could see them now, what would you say to make their day brighter? As you make your way back home there is someone you recognize outside that has a flat tire, are you willing to help them? What was their name again? What would you tell them and would you try to get to know them more? As you now make it into your house, you close the door and smile about the interactions you just had, feeling grateful there are people to connect with. Thank yourself for ushering kindness and compassion to the people you thought about helping and delighted in conversation today. You truly offer value in peoples lives. I AM FRIENDLY AND LOVED

MEDITATION FOR THE THIRD CHAKRA:

In a comfortable seated position, straighten your back by arching it slightly and lifting your chest high, roll your neck to get some flexibility in the shoulders. Be sure your sit bones are firmly planted, don't be afraid to move and lift the flesh around your thighs to make sure you feel firmly planted. Place the backs of your hands on the tops of your thighs, palms to the sky as you put your hands in Gian Mudra. First finger and thumb will touch at the tips making a zero while the other fingers stick out straight in front of them, stacked together. Take three long deep breaths, each one bringing you deeper into your body, each one relieving tension in the chest and back. Check your posture again, back straight, chest up, and chin slightly tucked in.

Bring your awareness to your navel (belly button) as you remember this was the connection to your mother, your lifeline that carried you to birth. As you focus on this area, visualize the color yellow as you allow creativity to blossom in your mind. We call upon the higher center of our being for healing the navel and bringing forth the drive and intensity to live life on purpose. Inhale long deep breaths and exhale the air completely from your lungs. Take another deep breath of creativity, hold the breath, 3, 2, 1, and exhale out the things people may think of you.

MEDITATION FOR THE FOURTH CHAKRA:

In a comfortable seated position, straighten your back by arching it slightly and lifting your chest high, roll your neck to get some flexibility in the shoulders. Be sure your sit bones are firmly planted, don't be afraid to move and lift the flesh around your thighs to make sure you feel firmly planted. Place the backs of your hands on the tops of your thighs, palms to the sky as you put your hands in Gian Mudra. First finger and thumb will touch at the tips making a zero while the other fingers stick out straight in front of them, stacked together. Take three long deep breaths, each one bringing you deeper into your body, each one relieving tension in the chest and back. Check your posture again, back straight, chest up, and chin slightly tucked in.

Bring your awareness to the center of your chest, focusing on your heartbeat. Visualize the color green as you imagine the heart pumping blood to all of your organs and emotionally opening up to bigger and brighter expressions. Place your hands over your heart,"calling upon the higher center of the body for grounded, diplomatic grace. There is an ask to for the heart to remain safely open and to continue to be a beacon for the right interaction in life". Take a deep loving breath in by expanding the chest as far as it will go, hold the breath, 3, 2, 1, and exhale, releasing heartache. Take another deep breath of compassion, hold the breath, 3, 2, 1, and exhale out negativity. Sit still as you witness the sensation you created, feel the energy used to wake the heart and keep it open.

MEDITATION FOR THE FIFTH CHAKRA:

In a comfortable seated position, straighten your back by arching it slightly and lifting your chest high, roll your neck to get some flexibility in the shoulders. Be sure your sit bones are firmly planted, don't be afraid to move and lift the flesh around your thighs to make sure you feel firmly planted. Place the backs of your hands on the tops of your thighs, palms to the sky as you put your hands in Gian Mudra. First finger and thumb will touch at the tips making a zero while the other fingers stick out straight in front of them, stacked together. Take three long deep breaths, each one bringing you deeper into your body, each one relieving tension in the chest and back. Check your posture again, back straight, chest up, and chin slightly tucked in.

Bring your awareness to your throat and the area between your ears and shoulders. While you focus, visualize the color blue as it cools and restores these area's of your body."Let's now ask the throat to speak how we truly feel inside and to use the voice when its most needed". Take a deep cool breath in, hold the breath, 3, 2, 1, and exhale, releasing untold stories. Take another deep breath of self confidence, hold the breath, 3, 2, 1, and exhale speculation.

MEDITATION FOR THE SIXTH CHAKRA:

In a comfortable seated position, straighten your back by arching it slightly and lifting your chest high, roll your neck to get some flexibility in the shoulders. Be sure your sit bones are firmly planted, don't be afraid to move and lift the flesh around your thighs to make sure you feel firmly planted. Place the backs of your hands on the tops of your thighs, palms to the sky as you put your hands in Gian Mudra. First finger and thumb will touch at the tips making a zero while the other fingers stick out straight in front of them, stacked together. Take three long deep breaths, each one bringing you deeper into your body, each one relieving tension in the chest and back. Check your posture again, back straight, chest up, and chin slightly tucked in.

Bring your awareness to the middle of your forehead, but slightly slower– the brow line. Keep your eyes closed as you turn you two eyes up to look at the brow. (If the eyes were open, you'd be cross eyed) Keep your closed eyes focused up as you visualize the color Indigo (deep royal blue) as you allow the strength of the eyes to create a new gaze. If you find your eyes get tired quickly, relax them and resume when you are ready, with time you'll be able to hold the posture longer. " Let's call upon the higher center of the mind to bring the foresight and internal sight needed to continue the path of self-knowledge". Take a refreshing breath in, hold the breath, 3, 2, 1, and exhale, releasing missed opportunity. Take another deep breath of trust, hold the breath, 3, 2, 1, and release self doubt.

SEVENTH CHAKRA SELF CARE & HEALING PRACTICES

Keeping the head covered as you practice this meditation will assist in protecting the energy at the top of the head. You may over time find yourself wanting to cover your head and this is a normal process with spiritual practice as many wear turbans, hats, and scarfs while in devotional practice or just moving about their day to protect the energy of the head and aura of the body. Working with this part of the body may increase awareness and understanding of the dream state. Recording what you experience and ideas that come to you greatly benefit the flow of energy. Meditation exercises will increase as the crown gets nurtured and supported with attention and protection.

MEDITATION FOR THE SEVENTH CHAKRA:

In a comfortable seated position, straighten your back by arching it slightly and lifting your chest high, roll your neck to get some flexibility in the shoulders. Be sure your sit bones are firmly planted, don't be afraid to move and lift the flesh around your thighs to make sure you feel firmly planted. Place the backs of your hands on the tops of your thighs, palms to the sky as you put your hands in Gian Mudra. First finger and thumb will touch at the tips making a zero while the other fingers stick out straight in front of them, stacked together. Take three long deep breaths, each one bringing you deeper into your body, each one relieving tension in the chest and back. Check your posture again, back straight, chest up, and chin slightly tucked in.

Bring your awareness to the top of your head, the area we never see, but it exposed to so much in life. As you focus your energy, visualize the color purple emanating from the top of your head like a lighthouse. "There is a call to he heavens for healing the crown and allowing the messages above to imprint the fabric of our life". Take a cosmic breath in, hold the breath, 7,6,5,4,3,2,1, and exhale, releasing everything you thought you knew. Take another deep breath of new life, hold the breath, 7, 6, 5, 4, 3, 2, 1, and release expectation. When complete, sit in silence to feel the energy you have just created and cleared from your life.

MEDITATION FOR BETTER COMMUNICATION

Communication is the lifeblood to our intrinsic understanding and ultimate reality. We use communication to bring our ideas together and reshape the narrative to be more understanding, diverse, and open to new ideas. Take a deep breath in, hold the breath, 3, 2, 1, and exhale.

Take a deep breath in, fill the bottom of your belly, then the top of the belly, then lungs and chest. Hold the breath for as long as you can and release it when you feel ready. Keep your eyes closed and bring the conversations you'd like to have to the forefront of your mind. Sit here and ruminate on the discussions, and issues you'd like to resolve. Take another deep breath and exhale through an open mouth. I LISTEN.

COMFORT IN CROWDS

As you sit in a comfortable seated position with the eyes closed, bring the attention to your style of being with people and how you like to recharge yourself. Taking moments to prepare yourself for the energy you are about to enter. A low toned place, low lighting and all the things you need. Changing our perception of a place before we go in, creating a positive experience before it happens can recreate the reality you step into– "May you always feel comfortable with who you are and the way you move in life. Take three long and deep inhale's and exhale's as you release tension from your shoulders and chest. I AM COMFORTABLE TO BE OUT IN PUBLIC.

TO FEEL MORE OUTGOING

Seated in a comfortable position with the eyes closed, bring your attention to how you hope to feel by being more apt to say yes when someone asks you out for fun. Focus on the images that come to mind when you think about how pleasurable it is to be with others and to be outside of your immediate environment. There is a lot of ease, smiles, and laughs to go around. Inhale deeply, hold the breath, 4, 3, 2, 1, exhale completely and hold the breath out, 4, 3, 2, 1, and inhale. You may relax. I ADORE ALL EXPERIENCES THAT MAKE ME FEEL FUN AND OUTGOING.

AUTHENTICITY

You wake up in the morning ready for life, knowing who you are and who you hope to become. You try hard to understand the larger meaning of your life and enjoy the process and perspectives it brings to your awareness. The diligence you apply to your practices get you to deeper aspects of what you truly believe, whether its right or wrong, you are right. Please close your eyes, take a deep breath in, fill the bottom of your belly, then fill your lungs, and exhale gently. Keeping your eyes closed, is there more about yourself you can express freely without regret? Are there messages being relayed? When you feel ready, take another deep breath, and exhale through an open mouth.

MEDITATION FOR ENJOYING YOUR BEAUTIFUL LIFE

In a comfortable seated position, straighten your back by arching it slightly and lifting your chest high, roll your neck to get some flexibility in the shoulders. Be sure your sit bones are firmly planted, don't be afraid to move and lift the flesh around your thighs to make sure you feel firmly planted. Place the backs of your hands on the tops of your thighs, palms to the sky as you put your hands in Gian Mudra. First finger and thumb will touch at the tips making a zero while the other fingers stick out straight in front of them, stacked together. Take three long deep breaths, each one bringing you deeper into your body, each one relieving tension in the chest and back. Check your posture again, back straight, chest up, and chin slightly tucked in.

Bring your awareness to the center of the chest and focus on the imagery of your heart. Watch your heart as it beats, sending blood to all the important vessels it supports. We put so many tasks on the heart and ask for its support. As you gaze upon it take a moment to shower your heart with love and compassion. Take a moment to thank your heart for guiding you to more empowering situations after feeling broken and abused. Today the heart will be recognized, as love is poured into its divine process. Today you are recognized as love is

221

poured into your divine process. Love is you, love is all around you, and you are loved.

Bring your awareness to your hands, as they are extensions of the heart. Rub the hands together vigorously using the friction to create heat. Place the heated hands over the heart and repeat, "I am love, love is all around me, and I am loved by others. I am love, love is all around me, and I am loved by others. I am love, love is all around me, and I am loved by others". You may release your hands, take a few cleansing breaths and relax. AND SO IT IS.

MEDITATION FOR INVOKING YOUR INNER SPIRIT

Today I sit here in all of my humble humility as an open vessel for love and guidance. I look to the heavens and understand there is more for me to experience. I look to the east as the Sun rises, I know there is another day upon me. I look to the west to witness the Sun set and the Moon illuminate and I am reminded how connected I am to life. I call upon my inner spirit to send me signs of love and synchronicity as I move throughout my life today, and everyday. May I be blessed to know that I am on the path and be aware enough to know when its happening for me. It is, and forever will be. Ase.

A PRAYER FOR THE INNER CHILD

Today I sit as the child I remember, innocent, wide eyed, and curious. I gaze upon me and smile as I remember how much I wanted to know, I really was an amazing kid, with an honest heart and an openness to learn. I remember vividly how innocent I was, how much I valued my safety and knew when someone was good for me. I will continue to take steps toward positive self discovery and remember that having a mind like a child only makes life more fun.

AN AFFIRMATION ON DEALING WITH PAIN

Today I honor myself because I notice I am uneasy. The uncomfortable feelings I have are because I need some time for myself, so I can work through what needs to be felt. I am strong even when I feel moments of weakness, and now is not a time of weakness, I feel these emotions because I am strong. What I feel on the inside cannot be seen outside of me, so when I hurt, I know I need to reach out to someone I trust. When I find myself in pain, I know that I am not alone. I honor who I am, how I feel and what got me here because I believe I can heal. It is and so it will be.

HEALING AFFIRMATION

The path to healing can be marked out with milestones and pitfalls along the way, however they are can be looked at as battle scars, proudly worn with honor. Everyone's journey to healing the self looks the different therefore I choose not to be a victim of my life, but rather a humble hero of my own making. Every tough time in life shows me another way to look at life and for that I feel grateful. Everyday I heal for love. I ask the higher powers that be to guide me safely through my journey of healing, always pointing me towards the way of soothing my senses, and to connect with those that will guide me to better solutions. IT IS AND SO IT WILL BE.

AFFIRMATION FOR BETTER ROUTINES

When I wake up for the day, I wake up to my life refreshed and ready to start a new day. When I wake up to my life I bring new energy, leaving what happened yesterday behind me. I take care to put awareness around the habits I'd like to transform. I enjoy being around people who allow me to be authentic and seek those relationships more and more each day. I take care to eat well when I am able to, I choose healthy options when they are offered, and I participate in the cooking of my own foods. I take pleasure in the way I provide and prepare nourishment for my body because it prepares me for a good life. When I get home from my day I take care to nourish the living things in my home and put in effort to refresh and prepare my environment for less stress and chaos. As I wind down and lay in bed I look up at the ceiling and catalogue how well my day went, sending blessings to those who need them, while thanking and loving myself for a day well done. I am excited to meet my dreams with openness and take pleasure in knowing another chance to make more out of my life is on the horizon. I love myself, my routine, and work hard to refine my process. My routines are perfect.

WATER MEDITATION

This is a meditation to bless your water before you consume it. When you take in this water that has been spoken to by your kind and loving words of intention and devotion, you take these words into your body. Pour a glass of water, one you can see through. Sit in a comfortable place with your spine straight and an open mind. Out loud you will say words of affirmation to your water and over time learn what it is you'd like to say and have permeate through your body. There is no right or wrong way, just practice the concept of loving kindness and your words will lead the way.

"I give so much thanks to this cool container filled with nourishment, minerals, and hydration. I love the way you hydrate me, it makes me feel young and alive. I take care not to waste you because I value your impact in my life. Today I will remember how important it is to honor you". Take a sip of your water and enjoy it as it passes your lips, graces your tongue, hits the back of your throat and eases slowly down the esophagus. Enjoy as you repeat the process knowing all that intention and appreciation is now entering and fulfilling your body.

FIRE MEDITATION

Fire is the element of desire and what we are meant to do with this life. It ignites us and makes the spirit courageous and ready to take on a new challenge. When you honor your fire, you give awareness to your creativity and that is what we intend to do in this meditation.

Please come into a comfortable seated position with the spine straight and the eyes closed. Inhale deeply for 5, 4, 3, 2, 1, and exhale completely. Inhale as you gather up all your worries and exhale. Visualize a flame on the top of a candle in the center of your heart, in the middle of your chest. Continue to breath deeply as you watch the flame dance around, become still, dim, and then dance again. Focus on size of the flame, can you make it larger? Make the flame as large as you can and let it burn hot. Inhale deeply, exhale completely. As you continue to focus on the flame, allow it to dim once again and finally allow it to go out. Check your posture, back straight, chin back, chest up and out. Inhale deeply, exhale completely as we begin breathing fire. Even breaths through the nose in and out as the belly mimics the nose. Inhale and the belly button is pushed out and exhale the belly button will be toward the spine. As you pump the belly, the air will flow in and out of the nostrils evenly, with time this will be effortless, don't try to hard, just let if flow. Inhale, exhale, inhale, exhale. Listen to the sound of your breath go in and out of your body as you imagine the navel as a hammer pumping against the spine and waking up the

226

creative center– solar plexus. Continue going, don't stop, try not to think just even inhale, exhale, inhale belly is extended, exhale and the belly is contracted and tight. 1 more minuet, you are doing great. INHALE, HOLD, 4, 3, 2, 1, EXHALE. Inhale again and hold, 3, 2, 1, and exhale. REPEAT: I honor my fire, I honor my creativity, I honor my fire, I honor my creativity, I honor my fire, I honor my creativity. Sit here for a moment as you behold the energy you have created with the fire in your belly. Remember that this exercise and area of your body is the lifeblood of creative self expression and the chance to create the Prana needed to live long and healthy days. You may relax.

GROUNDING ON EARTH

When you think of the earth, what comes to mind for you? Is it just the place you live or do you carry more stock into its purpose in your day to day? This meditation is to connect you to the large focus of what the earth is meant to teach us about ourselves. In a comfortable seated position please close your eyes and take a few long and deep cleansing breaths, inhale, exhale, good. Visualize your favorite place to take a walk, notice what draws your attention. The nature is pretty lively today, what animals do you see and what is the mood of the people around you if any? Inhale deeply, exhale completely. As you make your way, what else is particularly noticeable about your walk that you've never noticed before? As you take in the full view and landscape, how is the color? Focus on the colors in your minds eye, allow them to get as

227

vibrant as they can get. Walking along you see a huge patch of bright green, cool, damp, grass. Excited, you kick your shoes off and stand in the grasses glory sinking in the sun as you turn your smiling face to it. Open your hands at your side and allow the rays to hit your palms. Inhale deeply, exhale completely. Now begin to stomp your feet, and clap your hands as no one around you even notices what you are doing, they aren't looking your way as you continue to stomp, clap, smile and enjoy the earth's natural vibrational rhythm working inside you. As you slow your rhythm you come to a seated position on the grass to take in the energy you created and to bask in the suns rays for a little more time. As you sit with your eyes closed and spine straight you take in large, deep, cleansing breaths. Bring your awareness to the fact that you feel grounded at the base of your body, take notice how stable the ground feels beneath you and how good it feels under your feet. Take a few more long deep breaths as you bring your current awareness back to where you sit in the present moment. What are the smells and tastes you have now? Continue to inhale and exhale and when you feel ready you can relax and open your eyes. Take some time outside today or tomorrow if you can and recreate your dance with the earth.

MEDITATION ON YOUR CONNECTION TO THE GALAXY

In a comfortable seated position, straighten your back by arching it slightly and lifting your chest high, roll your neck to get some flexibility in the shoulders. Be sure your sit bones are firmly planted, don't be afraid to move and lift the flesh around your thighs to make sure you feel firmly planted. Place the backs of your hands on the tops of your thighs, palms to the sky as you put your hands in Gian Mudra. First finger and thumb will touch at the tips making a zero while the other fingers stick out straight in front of them, stacked together. Take three long deep breaths, each one bringing you deeper into your body, each one relieving tension in the chest and back. Check your posture again, back straight, chest up, and chin slightly tucked in.

Bring your awareness to the galaxy that conspires above you, the Sun, Moon, Mercury, Mars, Venus, all the personal planets circling around the ecliptic influencing how we feel and what we believe. As above so below, we feel the current of life as it shifts and changes. Imagine the planets circling around you as you sit in silence and peace. Inhale fully, exhale completely. As we narrow the focus we concentrate on the Sun, immediately we feel the warmth this planet gives off as we concentrate on its bright orange/yellow hue. A bright ball of fire starts the day, brings us light, makes food grow, and nourishes all bodies on the planet. The Sun brings with it the determination to begin another day, its what makes us realize we have a purpose and helps us realize what actions we must participate in order to make it happen. Lets take a deep breath in for the Sun and hold the breath, 5, 4, 3, 2, 1, and exhale allowing the belly to soften.

We now take our focus to the Moon, the way we process our life and the personalization we assign to ensure safety, comfort and emotional maturity. If you focus on the color of the Moon you realize the hue is metallic, silver, white, and sparkles if you look at it just right. In our perception depending on the day, we can see the Moon in its various cycles throughout month. From Lunation to Lunation we witness the Moons crescent as it wanes, allowing us to see what lacks and what needs attention. Then we watch the fullness unfold as waxes us to finish what we started, to end and old cycle and prepare for a new one. The Moon is our gracious teacher, giving us a new flavor each day as it makes its way through the Zodiac. Lets take a deep breath in for the Moon and hold the breath, 5, 4, 3, 2, 1, and exhale allowing the legs to soften. Stretch them out and get more comfortable if you feel ready.

Moving on to Mercury, the planet of communication, we realize its not easy to see the color of it, or to even know where it is in the sky if you aren't an avid sky watcher. No matter what, it travels closely to the Sun effecting our lives in the same kinds of cycles as the Moon as it makes its way through the Zodiac. It moves forward and backward through retrogrades, pausing to let us regroup and gather our thoughts before we move on to the next stage. Lets take a deep breath in for the Mercury and hold the breath, 5, 4, 3, 2, 1, and exhale allowing more space in the lungs. REPEAT: "Mercury, please give me the direction to make good choices in where to go and who to talk to", inhale deeply, exhale completely allowing even more room in the lungs.

We will now focus on Mars, the planet of war and our internal determination and motivations. Depending on the time of year, you may be able to see this big red ball of gas in the sky as it flavors our experience making its way through the signs of the Zodiac. Mars can give us determination and the will to stand up for ourselves and what we need to survive. Lets take a deep breath in for the Venus and hold the breath, 5, 4, 3, 2, 1, exhale relaxing all muscles in the face. REPEAT: "Mars, please give me the will to continue the fight and continue to light the path", inhale deeply, exhale completely releasing all tension from the head.

We now venture out to Venus, the planet of love and money. Just as Mercury it may be hard to see the color, but for some inexperienced sky watchers, Venus can still be visible to you. Depending on the time of year and where you are in the world, Venus can show up as a morning star or evening star, either rising before the Sun or setting before the Moon. It's one of the most advantageous planets as it gives us more to strive for. It's the planet that helps us identify what love is and what we need in order to feel satisfied with life. It's the planet that gives us the earning potential needed to gather the resources we are to share with others and save for the future. Lets take a deep breath in for the Venus and hold the breath, 5, 4, 3, 2, 1, exhale allowing more space in the heart. REPEAT: "Venus, please shine through me as I give love and share love, I welcome wealth to come my way", inhale deeply, exhale completely allowing even more room for the heart.

MEDITATION ON THE UNIVERSE

In a comfortable seated position, straighten your back by arching it slightly and lifting your chest high, roll your neck to get some flexibility in the shoulders. Be sure your sit bones are firmly planted, don't be afraid to move and lift the flesh around your thighs to make sure you feel firmly planted. Place the backs of your hands on the tops of your thighs, palms to the sky as you put your hands in Gian Mudra. First finger and thumb will touch at the tips making a zero while the other fingers stick out straight in front of them, stacked together. Take three long deep breaths, each one bringing you deeper into your body, each one relieving tension in the chest and back. Check your posture again, back straight, chest up, and chin slightly tucked in.

Bring your awareness to the galaxy that conspires above you, Saturn, Jupiter, Uranus, and Neptune, all circling around the ecliptic influencing our collective aim. As above so below, we feel the current of life as it shifts and changes. Imagine the planets circling around you as you sit in silence and peace. Inhale fully, exhale completely. As we narrow the focus we concentrate on the Saturn, the planet of time and change. Its what brings you to an understanding that all things come to an end and time moves us on to new experiences. Saturn ushers in the experience of maturation, rising to the higher points of your life so you can deliver your voice, your message, and gifts to society– filling the needs of the time. Lets take a deep breath in for the Saturn and hold the breath, 5, 4, 3, 2, 1, and exhale allowing the whole body to soften. REPEAT: "Saturn, please help me see the path to evolve ", inhale deeply, exhale completely and allow the body to sink deeper.

We will now focus on the actual giant in our solar system, Jupiter. It brings benevolence, higher thinking and makes things larger when next to them. Jupiter gives us a boost of positive motion and helps us have the courage to take risks to understand where extremes lie and where boundaries should be made. Jupiter not only makes things blissful, but gives a slap on the wrist when we are blind to what's in front of us. One of the last planets seen with the naked eye, Jupiter, is always there, pulsing, waiting for the moment to extend its energy to expand and enlarge your perspective, big or small. Jupiter is our benevolent teacher, when we learn all there is to know about reality, we are given new perspectives that help shape and elevate what we have learned–just when you think you know, you realize you have no idea. Lets take a deep breath in for Jupiter and hold the breath, 5, 4, 3, 2, 1, and exhale allowing the thoughts in you mind to soften to soften. REPEAT: "Saturn, please help me see the path to evolve ", inhale deeply, exhale completely and soften the tension around thoughts in your mind.

We will now lend our attention to Uranus, the harbinger of unexpected realties, and one of the last planets to be discovered. Uranus is a gaseous planet that is large and full of surprise as it brings an err energy that forces you to upgrade or refine a situation that has been outgrown. Uranus is a slow moving planet, giving the intellect time to fully grasp a concept by thinking of ways to slightly improve it or make it work specifically for you. Uranus is here to make our communication exquisite and to jolt us into actions that benefit the whole. Lets take a deep breath in for the Uranus and hold the breath, 5, 4, 3, 2, 1, and exhale allowing the thoughts in you mind to soften to soften. REPEAT: "Uranus, please help me see the path as I remove my personal motivations to the side ", inhale deeply, exhale completely and soften the tension around your jaw and in your mouth.

Lastly we will focus on the outermost planet of the solar system, Neptune. Another gaseous planet, it lies on the exterior realms of the galaxy, but represents the exterior realms of our mind. Neptune gives us the focus to see outside of our reality and extends to realities that encompass us all as one, not separate. Neptune shows us where our talents lie and how we can best serve the collective consciousness. It is the planet that represents overall happiness in life and the meaningful steps to get there. Lets take a deep breath in for the

234

Neptune and hold the breath, 5, 4, 3, 2, 1, and exhale allowing the thoughts in you mind to soften to soften. REPEAT: "Neptune, please show me how to best serve the world and myself for ultimate happiness ", inhale deeply, exhale completely, and so It is.

MEDITATION FOR THOSE WHO HAVE PASSED ON

This meditation is a loving tribute to the people you love dearly that have departed the earth or are anticipated to leave soon. Before closing your eyes, remember that you are loved, safe and the emotions that come into your awareness are merely there to help you see how important your connection truly was. If you have any photos or mementos you'd like to set out for this meditation, now is the time. Sit in a position you enjoy being in whether its correct posture or not. Please close your eyes and inhale as an image of the person you love so much comes into your awareness, tell them hi as they show you what it is they would like for you to remember, not the images of pain, but the images of joy. Recollect a memory you feel was most enjoyable between the two of you and engage deeply. Take in any nostalgic smells or tastes that come to mind as you spend time with your dearly departed. Now is the time to tell them something you haven't had the chance to say, what is it? Go ahead and speak it out loud and when you are finished take a long deep inhale and hold the breath, 5, 4, 3, 2, 1, exhale out with an open mouth. Again inhale and hold the breath, 5, 4, 3, 2, 1, dramatically exhale out with an open mouth. REPEAT: "I honor you in my practice today as I remember all the beautiful times we've shared together. While not perfect, I cherish what we had and I thank you for being in my life", inhale deeply, exhale completely, and so It is.

MEDITATION FOR HEALTHY RELATIONSHIPS

This meditation is for those who feel the need to improve the dynamic in the relationships they belong to, whether it be friendship, romantic or familial, we play an important roll in each one and this meditation is to help bring more to the table for each one. Please find a comfortable seated position that is free from interruption. Close your eyes and begin taking long deep inhale's and exhale's as you center yourself, with each inhale you feel your body expand, and with each exhale you sink deeper into your body, noticing each subtle feeling of comfort achieved. You will now visualize the person you'd like to strengthen a relationship with keep the image of them in your head as you recollect why you feel it needs work, think back to the situations that made it apparent your relationship needs elevation. As your mind scans to any images that are unsavory or memories that make you feel heated, take a deep inhale and slowly exhale– breath through any painful moments as you take full stock of your connection, its importance, and the reason you are sitting here today. Slow the mind down a bit as you remove your concentration from the person and direct your attention to your heart.

Visualize a small plant growing at the base of your heart, take a moment to water it and watch it grow. REPEAT: "I love you with all of your imperfections and I know you love me for mine, that is what makes this a divine connection". Take a long deep inhale and hold the breath, 5, 4, 3, 2, 1, exhale as slowly as you can. Again, inhale and hold the breath, 5, 4, 3, 2, 1, and exhale the breath making a hissing sound with the mouth.

AFFIRMATION TO EMBRACE WHERE YOU ARE

I honor the process I find myself in today as I realize there is more I'd like to feel from within. My experience does not revolve around external gratification, but one of internal satisfaction and delicate focus towards my bright and expansive future. I imagine who I will be once I am complete and polished, knowing deep down however, I never will be, I wonder where my life will decide to turn next? As I implement small incremental changes, I notice the distance I've gone to get to this place– a long road and there is no turning back. Self development is more than a diet or morning routine that touts a perfect life, its developing one's emotional and mental state so it is prepared for chaos should it ensue. Its putting the steps in place so I continue to rise. While learning new processes, I find out which one looks best on me, I don't follow dogma or the paths of other people, I follow my own unique process.

MEDITATION TO ESTABLISH EQUILIBRIUM

Please sit a comfortable seated position and close your eyes. We are working on balance– balance towards where our energy and mental faculties are spent. With your eyes closed, begin to visualize a scale, its gold with a sturdy base and two large plates, one on each side. Imagine putting all of your our goals, aspirations and hopes for the future on one side of the scale, what happens? If we take a full experience, from beginning to end by interpreting its reality to be a bad one and put experience on one side of the scale, nothing else, where would you find yourself? Take into your minds eye that the scale must constantly move on each side. One will become heavier than the other weighing it down and showing its impact so that you will easily notice when more needs to be added to the other side. Keep watching the scales move up and down evenly– this is a representation of the duality or polarity of life. When we absorb both sides we get the highest expression to come forth. Taking the example above as a positive, but uncomfortable experience even though plans fell through or chaos ensued, we have to come to grips that more occurred out of that experience, something that is to be learned from or harnessed for strength. Take a long deep inhale and hold the breath, repeat the word balance 3 times, and exhale as slowly as you can. Again, inhale and hold the breath, 5, 4, 3, 2, 1, and exhale completely. And so it is.

HONORING THE SERPENT OF THE KUNDALINI

Today I honor the 7 energy centers in my body because I am fully aware of what they're about, where they are located in my body and what they are meant to do for me. My root chakra supports the base of my body where it all begins, helping me release my mental blockages around the past and where Im meant to be. My sacral chakra gives my body balance through aligning with my sexuality. It is here where my digestion gives me a head start, not only do I process the nutrients of my body here, but this is where my mental digestion starts to take place, where I begin to understand where I was and where I am headed. My solar plexus chakra aids in the breath given to life, it is where Prana and Apana live– the inhale and the exhale. When the breath is followed, listened for, and cultivated life blooms. Creation manifests as completed goals, creative self expression, and confidence. Projection LIVES HERE. My heart chakra keeps me open and vulnerable, ready to display the capacity to let go and allow someone to know me, so they may learn how to love me. My throat chakra controls my voice and contribution in physical form. It is where my authenticity shines through and I express who "self" is to others. I speak my peace and give others an ear. This is the place I LISTEN. My third eye is a special place, it is the eye that sees behind the eyelids when closed. It is where my sense of direction comes from and where my intuition is acted out. I see beyond what my two eyes see, I see who I am on the inside. My crown chakra is where I

239

receive the messages from the outer world to complete my inner world. It is the place where no thinking happens, no knowing happens, no-thing happens– its where I go to "be". All of my chakras work together to make me a whole human being with the desire to expand my consciousness. Awakening the Kundalini awakens my consciousness and opens the world as I know it to states I could never dream of achieving. I was made for this journey and the journey is mine.

AFFIRMATION ON POSITIVITY

I am a strong, motivated person, what gets me moving in life is the promise of something more. Motivation comes when work is to be done, when my heart is truly in it and a sense of purpose has been understood. I realize there are times of rest and I cannot mistake these times for being unmotivated, these are times of rest and processing. However, when I'm done putting together my plan and I let go of judging my progress, I am propelled forward. Getting off the couch is much easier now because the light is showing brightly at the end of the tunnel. I am ready to walk into the life I dream of everyday. As I sit in places I'd rather not be, I gestate my passion in life and turn it into aspiration. I am not limited by my circumstances, I am limited by the capacity to see my freedom. The less I tie myself to material objects or specific places to be, the more freedom I achieve. Freedom is truly endless opportunity of choice. I'm able to choose any direction, you are free. I am motivated by my freedom, my limitless ability to move around the world and the endless experiences I am meant to have.

MEDITATION ON DREAMS

This meditation is to shine a light on the larger meanings to not feeling confident with who you are. Identifying when it is felt, what it looks like, and when it crops up are all a part of getting to higher states of emotional intelligence. As you think about yourself as a unique individual with a set of fingerprints all your own, DNA that could never be replicated and an expression that could not be replicated even if you were born on the same day, you start to realize that your whole life experience is one of sovereignty. Your life is not signified by how similar you can make yourself to be to other people. Its true that being authentic and confident feels like a risk, it can be a risk of not wanting to be rejected or possessing large amounts of fear around not being accepted or received. The idea is not to change exactly who you are at this moment, but instead to take small steps towards opening up to your confident life expression. It takes people a long time to develop certain unwanted habits and for some, it may take just as long to change them. Where you fall is unique for your life and for a brief moment in this meditation you will get a chance to uplift your confidence.

In a comfortable seated position, straighten your back by arching it slightly and lifting your chest high, roll your neck to get some flexibility in the shoulders. Be sure your sit bones are firmly planted, don't be afraid to move and lift the flesh around your thighs to make sure you feel firmly planted. Place the backs of your hands on the tops of your thighs, palms to the sky as you put your hands in Gian Mudra. First finger and thumb will touch at the tips making a zero while the other fingers stick out straight in front of them, stacked together. Take three long deep breaths, each one bringing you deeper into your body, each one relieving tension in the chest and back. Check your posture again, back straight, chest up, and chin slightly tucked in.

Bring your awareness situation that left you in a state of not feeling confident. What were you doing and what were you trying to accomplish at that moment? Is there a logical explanation to why you don't feel confident? Take a deep inhale 3, 2, 1, and exhale slowly. Take your attention away from what doesn't make you feel confident and instead put your focus towards what does. What are you wearing when you walk in your essence? Visualize yourself walking down the street with your head held high, wearing your most prized possessions, feeling healthy and on track with your routines and excited for where your adventure will land you for the day. You don't have a care in the world because you are not concerned with anything anyone thinks about you. When people say hello as they pass you, you warmly show all teeth and grin and reply with an exuberant "hello, have a great day". You exude what it means to be a present and engaged with life, prepared to take on challenge and chaos should it show its ugly head. AND SO IT IS.

SEEING YOURSELF IN A NEW SPACE

This **is** a meditation to imagine where in the world you should be. Are you wondering if there is somewhere else you'd like to live or work? Is there a location in your minds eye that represents what it means to be in paradise and what is paradise to you? In a comfortable seated position, straighten your back by arching it slightly and lifting your chest high, roll your neck to get some flexibility in the shoulders. Be sure your sit bones are firmly planted, don't be afraid to move and lift the flesh around your thighs to make sure you feel firmly planted. Place the backs of your hands on the tops of your thighs, palms to the sky as you put your hands in Gian Mudra. First finger and thumb will touch at the tips making a zero while the other fingers stick out straight in front of them, stacked together. Take three long deep breaths, each one bringing you deeper into your body, each one relieving tension in the chest and back. Check your posture again, back straight, chest up, and chin slightly tucked in.

Bring your awareness to the first place your mind focuses on that to you, represents your sense of freedom, the place the brings you the greatest joy when you lay your eyes upon it. Now that you see the place, lets expand on it some more. Inhale deeply, exhale completely. What are the colors you witness in your visualization? Is there a color that sticks out to you the most? Would it happen to match any of your chakra centers? If this vision takes place outside, focus on what the weather like and how does it feels on your skin. Look up, take view of the sky and its movements. If this vision takes place inside, what is the temperature of the room and are you comfortable? Take a seat next to the nearest window and look up to take a view of the sky and what moves above your head. Imagine what your life would look like in this space all the time, living and breathing in your idea of paradise. Take a moment to go through your regular routine in this space and if you need to adjust what you do for a living to make it work to your advantage. What kinds of foods are at your disposal for nourishment? Are there activities you can enroll your self in or communities you can join? Who is living next to you and how do you interact with each other? Think about how you will effect change in this new place and the people you will come across. Consider the new or expanded love within your relationships and being in love with your life. Take a long deep inhale and hold the breath, REPEAT the words "everyday I get closer to paradise" 3 times, and exhale as slowly as you can. Again, inhale and hold the breath, 5, 4, 3, 2, 1, and exhale completely. And so it is.

MEDITATION ON VISUALIZING

Take a deep breath in, hold for 5 seconds, and exhale. Visualize yourself perched on top of a small grassy hill. The wind is blowing and you can feel the hairs on your head move around rapidly. The smell of sweet flowers graces the wind as it gently blows past your sensitive nose. Catching a butterfly in the near distance you realize you are sitting in a place with the perfect view. Off into the horizon is a span of mountain ranges, valleys, and mesas as far as the eye can reach in a full 360 degree view. Suddenly the sky falls dark and every star in the galaxy creates pinholes across a black backdrop for you to gaze upon. As you sit in silence and wonderment the sky changes from day to night over and over while you gaze upon cloudless sky's and take the moonlit path of the night. Take a few more moments here to bask in the glory of what you are witnessing in your minds eye. Take a nice long deep breath and bring your awareness back to this present moment, and exhale. Inhale again and hold the breath, 3, 2, 1, and exhale.

MEDITATION FOR MOVING ON

Take a safe, quiet, seated position and close your eyes. Imagine the memories you'd like to leave behind as you realize there is a big box to the right of your sight. You go over to it and place the past memories inside the box. Any negative thought patters around the past goes into the box, standing there, you carefully analyze your life and the experiences your mind ruminates on that does not help you progress. As you look down at the box, exhausted from searching, you realize its getting full. Neatly close the box and use the tape beside it to fasten the top shut. Take the box with you to the river you hear down the way. As you stand at the shore with your box full of memories gently place the box in the water and allow the river's current sweep away the memories of the past. Keep your eyes on the box until you are no longer able to see it. Inhale deeply and exhale completely. Inhale again, taking in fresh unburdened energy, and exhale the air out of the lungs completely as you bring your awareness to the present moment.

A MEDITATION TO CLEANSE YOUR HOUSE

Light an incense, scented candle, or your favorite resin to give burned offering. As you light it repeat "today I cleanse my home with good intention and honest faith, please guide me and my space toward protection". As you walk to each corner of your house, wave your burned offering and repeating "I bless this house, I bless my life" and continue to slowly and intentionally scan your home addressing any corners or areas that feel as if they need refreshment. When you are complete you may allow the rest of the item you chose to burn freely as you open your doors and windows for at least 2 minuets. Allow the cleansing process to finish by ushering the heavy energies out of your space.

*Cleansing any dishes, dumping trash and putting away misplaced items will increase the free flowing energy to move through your home.

A MEDITATION FOR DREAMS

Please close your eyes and sit in a comfortable

seated position before you make your way to bed. This meditation is to help your subconscious mind open before you lay your head down to sleep. As you sit here take long deep breaths in and out. Inhale, exhale, inhale, exhale, bring your eyes to focus at your brow (you will be cross eyed) as you look at the Third Eye. Stay here as you continue to take long inhale's and exhale's. If your eyes start to feel tired, take a break and resume the posture when you feel ready. Inhale fully and exhale completely. Bring your eyes to a restful position as they remain closed. You will now listen to these words and take them into your being, believe them, know them and sink into them. It is your sleep mantra that connects you to the ethereal dream world. "Tonight I ask for the memory of my dreams. Tonight I ask for understanding to what occurs when I am unconscious. May I be blessed every night to explore the depths of who I am through traveling and experiencing the adventures in the corners of my mind. May I always be protected. And so it is". Take a moment to continue your stillness as your cells try to catch up with your requests. If you can remember to ask each night before you fall asleep, you will realize more often than not, your ask will come true.

MEDITATION FOR AWARENESS
In a comfortable seated position, straighten your back slightly and lift your chest high. Be sure your sit bones are firmly planted. Place the backs of your hands on the tops of your thighs, palms to the sky as you put your hands in Gian Mudra. First finger

and thumb will touch at the tips making a zero while the other fingers stick out straight in front of them, stacked together. Take three long deep breaths, each one bringing you deeper into your body, each one relieving tension in the chest and back. Check your posture again, back straight, chest up, and chin slightly tucked in. Inhale deeply and exhale completely.

Bring your awareness to the wholeness of your journey so far. Are there things you've realized about yourself that feel enlightening now? Ruminate on one that brings you to a state of freedom and release. Here is where you'll take a moment to give your attention to states of being that have given you the most education about yourself, what have you learned this far? Feel in your heart as these words reach your ears, "I am grateful to the journey ahead of me and the one that lays behind, I feel changed and enlivened by the way I process my life and I look forward to many more years of discovery". And so it is. You may stay here for as long as you need, being sure to give yourself space to digest what comes up.

MEDITATION FOR GROUNDING INTO YOUR PRACTICE

As you sit in a comfortable position anywhere you choose, close your eyes and sink into a nice quiet space. Raise your shoulders up to your ears and drop them back to your sides. Roll your head to stretch your neck a few times to get more settled. Take long deep breaths, try your best to allow thoughts to pass, its okay to have thoughts. Stay here as you continue to take deep inhale, long exhale. Inhale, slowly exhale, focus on the breath. Now begin to visualize yourself doing your practices, one after another, day after day, your consistency shines through. Stay here to continue watching your life improve from the small steps you are taking. Remember to include waking up on time to start them and the benefits of being prepared for your life each day. Ruminate on this. Take a deep breath in of possibility, hold the breath, 3, 2, 1, and exhale, releasing doubt. Take another deep breath of grounded practices, hold the breath, 3, 2, 1, and exhale all of the previous failed attempts.

MEDITATION ON YOU

As you stand in front of the mirror, get close and observe the pupils of your eyes. Do you recognize the eyes staring back at you? How have you changed physically? Observe the face you may not look at in this way. Notice every freckle, scar, imperfection, and perfection you see. Take full stock in who you see yourself to be.

Take yourself to a comfortable place and sit in a position that works best for you. As you close your eyes, take 3 cooling and cleansing breaths to center yourself. Visualize the person you saw in the mirror a moment ago, what is this person doing now? Keep visualizing yourself moving through your day to day, does it look different than what you do now? Find yourself fitting into the space you'd like to see yourself in and where you would like to be. Find yourself with freedom, wealth, and knowledge to make better decisions. Place your hands over your heart, "may I continue to see myself and continue grow as a healthy and spiritual being", now place your hands in prayer pose and sit here to ponder for as long as you wish.

MEDITATION FOR WHOLENESS

Fullness of life is all around me, seeing what is in store, the bigger picture of it all. I live for all the moments that are unknown and I am unrestrained through my freedom of choice. Imagine a door at the end of a tunnel covered in plant life, wild flowers, and a sense of untamed wildness– it's a door to new opportunity. As you step through the door you realize there are things you've never seen before and you stop to take a look at the first place you notice. What is that place?

Please close your eyes, take a deep breath in, take it to the bottom of your belly, then fill your lungs. Hold for as long as you can and release it in peace. YOUR LIFE IS FULL.

MEDITATION ON THE FUTURE

I look towards the future as I digest what's happened to me in the past. I am a polished, forward thinking, and radiant human being. I am not my experiences, I am the perception of what I believe my journey is. I open a window to clear my energy, take in the fresh air and face toward a new outlook. The horizon looks bright and I feel good that I am not limited by my circumstances.

Please close your eyes, take a deep breath in, fill the bottom of your belly, then fill your lungs. Hold for as long as you can and release it in peace. Keep your eyes closed and envision words on a paper tucked away inside a box. As you open this box you realize the words on the paper say words you've always wanted to see for yourself, what does it say? AND SO IT IS.

MEDITATION TO RISE

There are two paths you find yourself looking upon. One of them leads to something you've always wanted, but when it you get it, that's it, you have nothing else to look forward to– your life still remains the same. The other path leads you to a road of unlimited potentiality, you'll just never get the choice. Everything will be spontaneous, forever changing, and unplanned. While hard, you realize life has a lot to offer when you go with the flow. As you align with new parts of yourself and revamp your beliefs. Which path shall you choose, staying the same or change?

Please close your eyes, take a deep breath in, fill the bottom of your belly, then fill your lungs. Hold for as long as you can and release you're breath quietly. Keep your eyes closed and envision what its like to have more than you ever thought you could because you opened fully to what life had in store. Sit here for a moment and feel it deep within you as you take another deep breath. RISE TO

YOUR LIFE.

MEDITATION FOR TRUTH

I honor the virtue inside of me as I realize everyone on this earth is inherently good. I am honest with myself because I search for my own internal self knowledge. The more honest I get with myself, the more I understand of others– my compassion comes from within and extends to everything around me.

Please close your eyes, take a deep breath in, fill the bottom of your belly, then fill your lungs. Hold for as long as you can and release it with an open mouth while you exhale a cleansing breath. Keep your eyes closed and envision a bright green light in the center of your chest, watch it emanate past your chest and surround your body creating a bright aura of gorgeous natural green energy. Stay here as you extend this aura 100 feet, keeping this bright glow in your minds eye for as long as possible. Feel it deep within you as you take another deep breath and exhale. HONESTY WITH YOURSELF IS YOUR GIFT THIS LIFETIME.

MEDITATION ON BEING A CHANNEL

This is a transmission to guide you in unlocking your intuitive response to your inner most desires. I hold the keys to my success today and everyday, so what does that success look like to me?

As you stay here a wile to contemplate, try your best to understand how you might get to this place. Do you struggle to start because you have fear around attaining an end goal? What do you honestly feel holds you back from what is truly desired?

Please close your eyes as you take a deep inhale. Contemplate about the messages that came to you while keeping compassion in your heart for your very unique process. NEVER STOP LISTENING.

MEDITATE ON INNER PEACE

My inner peace comes from the quiet spaces I find myself in. Where I feel the comfort of my world through the warmth on my skin, a satisfied belly, and just enough to make it work in my favor. I understand that I control my sense of inner peace through my practices, connection to my body and achieving brief states of a still and calm mind. No one can take this peace, no one can change this peace, I control my sense of inner peace.

Please close your eyes while you take 3 long deep inhales and exhales. Hold each inhale for as long as you can before exhaling. Imagine a park bench in the middle of a highway, cars rushing by you as your eyes are closed, all you can hear are birds chirping, don't they sound beautiful? YOU CONTROL YOUR SENSE OF INNER PEACE

MEDITATIVE AFFIRMATION FOR THE FULL MOON

As the moon waxes to its fullest potential, expanding its energetic frequencies, it comes to its final destination at the full moon phase. You are created as a human that is a lunation of influence, easily becoming the brightest star in the room and eventual leader of the group. The newest idea is always just coming to light, while frustrating at times, it's understood that anything worth having is worth waiting for– consciousness, in its full manifestation, takes time. This phase makes you feel impatient about the need for things to happen "now" , and confusion often sets in when the direction of an idea is lost or without vision. However, these feelings usually don't last long because you are not a person to remain in energy that doesn't align with higher values.

You are best understood well and received by others by establishing connections and expressing your freshly developed perceptions of life, remaining hopeful, ready to digest, and detached from outcome. Connecting with others is a cathartic process. But this catalog of brand-newness won't exactly mesh with some of your long held beliefs and disruption creates feelings of discomfort until the final vision comes into focus.

You see with clarity that can only come from shining a light directly on something, this full moon phase brings your thoughts and feelings to solid ground. The light being cast has a simple purpose for you– in order to gain a better understanding of where you are going– you need an open view of where you currently stand. Those who surround you, the environments you find yourself in and the information you consume are of high importance and contain facets of life that seem larger than one could imagine. Intensity and chaos follow you as "blind" external forces are drawn to your light. What better way to see in the dark than by the light of an incredible full moon?

Your full moon delivers more than one aspect of change, it includes parts that are painful, unjust, and can feel as large as death. Dramatics are never far from your experience as the polarity of life pulls you from one extreme to the next– whether it be a hardship or a blessing. Separation is a common theme as life plays out and you often look around to find that all the people you once knew are either gone from your life or have changed for the better. You are constantly pushed to seek out the best practices of life, and fiercely willing to leave behind what no longer serves the greater parts of who you are becoming.

Emotionally, this phase will have you feeling the deep contrast of the ebbs and flows of life in an extreme sense. Swaying violently from one frame of thought to another will always be a challenge. It is up to you to decide which is the best side to choose– in the end it's realized the balance of both is necessary. It's often hard to hold back feelings or expressions because you wear your heart on your sleeves, your feelings are hard felt, and seen from miles away.

Your full moon personality is largely influenced by relationships and their dynamics. Whether being in a successful and loving relationship or "divorcing", understanding what you want in the end is the goal– the larger questions will always be asked, "should I stay or should I go?. Constantly thinking about the "other" in life takes up a lot of mental space, as you fantasize dynamics, events, and conversations before they even occur. This yearning is healthfully nurtured as you move toward realistic experiences you find and build upon.

The separation of the sun and moon is the definition of a full moon event, it creates an intense desire to be close to another and is a main focal point to life. Over identification with relationships disrupts confidence and feelings of selfhood. Over time you've learned that your personal needs should be met by you first and is one of the most important and effective steps toward a healthy relationship with a full moon person.

Whether you are searching for transformation or avoiding its presence, you understand it's the only constant in life– nothing stays the same. You embrace change and that means you possess the control over your narrative. Questions full moon people ask is "are you a person that prefers to take the initiative, or do you wait for others to make decisions for you?" This cycle breeds fierce independence and will make you embrace your need to separate and take charge of what has made you feel dependent in the past– continued strength comes from autonomy.

The decision to impart on a new adventure becomes evident in this phase. Instituting new habits, releasing old attitudes or people and embracing new concepts come to a head when under this influence– this is where the potential of life is noticed. The potential of what could be, the ideas surrounding an end goal and the willingness to take risk get stronger the more you adapt. You may not always act on your impulses, but identifying a purpose allows your ideas to swirl and carefully create a course of action that works. You find that leaving old ideas behind may be challenging as new processes need space.

As the moon passes this phase and moves into the waning energy of the moon's cycle, you soon start to realize the small details and steps it will take to make your dreams come true. When the moon waxes we create organic structures around our ideas after we spend our time diligently working with the waning moon to tear down what is old and outdated.

The full moon ushers in unwavering energy that lasts long after the event takes place, showering you with a lunar concentration of energies that push you to find your way in the dark, to expose all that has been hidden, and to dig up what has been out of sight for far too long. You are brought to awareness by seeing what has been avoided and you cleverly come up with methods to improve– illumination and enlightenment are sought after attributes in an every day full moon experience. You are the essence of sight beyond sight.

YOGIC BREATHING TECHNIQUES: ALTERNATE NOSTRIL BREATHING

Sitting in a comfortable seated position, with your left hand on your knee, you will use the right hand to take the thumb and cover your right nostril. Cover the right nostril and inhale through the left nostril, switch nostrils using the ring finger to cover the left nostril to exhale out of the right nostril. Again you will inhale through the right nostril, switch fingers and use the thumb to close the right nostril and exhale out of the left. You are basically taking turns inhaling and exhaling through each nostril. * Do this cyclical breathing for 1 minuet. When complete, sit in silence to feel the energy you have just created.

YOGIC BREATHING TECHNIQUES: COOLING THE BODY AND SENSES

Sit in a comfortable seated position with the spine upright. The back is straight, the chest is up and the chin is slightly tucked in. You will close your eyes and take a few long deep breaths. Fix your mouth into the shape of the letter O as you inhale cool breaths through the mouth and exhale through the nose– you may close your mouth as you exhale if you wish. Inhale cool breath from open mouth and exhale warm air from the nostrils.

*Do this for 3 minutes and include it in your day anytime you need to cool off from hot temperatures or attitudes. Can be done with eyes open in stressful situations such as driving or before test taking.

BONUS AFFIRMATIONS

We are always in a state of becoming, life is but a series of miraculous unfoldings. Be present in the moment, aware of your breath, aware of your body, aware of the thoughts as they move through your mind. Enjoy the process and where it takes you.

Your Source given talents are guiding you. Whatever you create from that place in your chest - art, writing, food, music, love - is coming through you from a much more magical place. You are bringing Source into the material realm. Nothing made from the heart is in vain, it is a reflection of your deepest knowing. Your purpose lies in doing what you love.

Opportunity, like sewage, will rise to the surface. Some will turn their noses up, unwilling to do the hard work because they are turned away by the smell. Others will recognize that diligence is required and will do what is needed to clean up the mess. There will be moments when an opportunity comes disguised as sewage - not to make life hard, but to deter those that aren't worthy of the prize. Work to stay in energy of gratitude so that you may have the awareness to accept the gifts the Universe sends you.

Pour a glass of water. Hold it between warm palms and repeat: "like this water may I flow where I am needed, do the work of Source, and cleanse what is no longer needed. I drink this water in gratitude for all that I am given." Energetically take on the receptive properties of your prayer as you drink the glass of water.

Know that you are already where you are meant to be. The Universe conspires in your favor at all times. Look for the energy in your words, notice the intent in your actions. If things seem to be piling up against you, are you listening to the whispers of Source? Inhale a deep, hold for 4 counts and exhale as slowly as you can. Is there a message you hear or feel?

Live your life with pure intention. As you venture out into the world each day, your energy proceeds you. If your energy is angry, the world will reflect your anger back to you as you interact with others. If you move forward in love you will receive the same in return. Not every person will react in kind to you immediately, but in time you will have restructured your very essence. Eventually, you will live the life you have always dreamed of living.

Picture yourself living your most realized life. Now sink into the feeling that living life gives you. On a small piece of paper write down the way it makes you feel. Are you happy? Does the image feel authentic? Place this small note in a place where you have to look at least twice a day so that you stay present with the reality you wish to create.

Our expansive galaxy is a reflection of the Universe within. Cells glow like stars, each of our organs has a purpose for our health like planets, and the vast nebula flows like life-giving blood. Float in the soothing darkness, and know that you are cradled by nebula as a mother cradles her newborn babe.
As Above. So Below.

Light the fire of passion that lives within you. Become a flame that shines bright in the darkness. Lead the way for those that have yet to feel their heat.

Move and experience the smallest pleasures of your existence. Relish a breeze across your cheek, a sunray on your skin, let ice melt slowly on your tongue, or listen to an early morning bird song. Life is a magical world full of many subtle experiences.

You are Source manifest - a work of art and a reflection of your spiritual connection. Awaken your heart by showing others your vulnerability, there is strength in the beauty of your soul. Trust that your heart will be lovingly held both here in the physical as well as in Source's loving embrace.

Life can feel like forcing your feet into shoes that are two sizes too small. It's painful and eventually, we are forced to find shoes that fit our feet and our style anyway. Like most shoe shopping experiences, we try on different pairs, measure for proper fit, and do a little dance as a test before we commit to our purchase. Know that the same applies to life. We are allowed to "try on" life until we find our favorite fit. Permit yourself to find your most magical fit by being yourself.

Let go of having to be productive. "Doing" is as addictive as any substance on Earth. The body needs rest to heal, the soul needs silence to integrate emotions and the mind needs quiet to receive messages from Source. Take time to go within, listen to your breathing, and surrender to the idea that just being is an integral part of doing.

Our physical reality is a manifestation of our thoughts. How we perceive the world is colored by our experiences and by the emotions attached to them. It seems impossible to stay in a positive vibration when the world around us is in chaos, but that is exactly how we create change - by envisioning what has not yet happened. As our reality begins to align, we must be prepared for major shifts, not all of them will be positive in the beginning but as we move forward in our resolve we strengthen our power to change the narrative.

Our days can seem challenging. We feel pulled down by so many small things not turning out the way we'd like - it almost turns into a game of "what can go wrong today". There is another game we can play, one that's not so obvious and takes time to appreciate. This game has simple rules - as we proceed through life from a place of gratitude we begin to notice, slowly at first, how many things align in our favor. Each step of the way, we begin to see Source in our lives through signs, symbols, and synchronicities. Notice the clues!

The human body is a wondrous machine. Capable of many physical marvels, it also contains a highly technical early warning alarm system. When we maintain calm and conscious energy, we can feel when our energy is out of alignment, and what our body naturally wants to correct itself. Listen to your body now, Is there something you feel needs adjustment?

There are parts of ourselves that we wish to ignore. Those things we say or do that feel out of our control and are usually not well received. All parts of self need to be explored and expressed equally. New age spirituality leads us towards love and light although many of us have places inside cloaked in darkness. No one part is more important than any other. Give room to the shadows, most often than not this is where our greatest gifts are hidden.

Each one of us is born protected. As we emerge from our mothers we are strong and full of the knowledge that Source loves us. Although, as we grow and our lives venture, we forget that we are the children of the Universe. Please know that we are able, at any time, to call on that love. The seed remains whole inside of us, especially when buried under hatred, anger, and fear. Move through the world secure in knowing that with the slightest watering that seed will grow.

Hold fast to the truth that you are infinite energy having a human experience. You know very little about the Universe you live in. Remain flexible in your beliefs while remaining firm in the knowledge that Source is with you always.

Markers on the journey towards self-realization come in many forms. One of the most evident is the shedding of loved ones. As the hard work we put in begins to manifest, there will be those that are not on the same path. A transition begins to take place, and we search wildly for the meaning behind the disconnections. Find solace in the process. You are making space for and finding your people. The beautiful ones that will love and support you on the next leg of your travels as you adventure and discover yourself.

Everyone has a different idea of what is valuable; gold, jewels, possessions, money, and love. But these material possessions are but a representation of time. We all have access to it--time to spend, time to share, and time to waste. If we don't have time then we're out of time or we find our time is up-- not realizing it goes quickly. Be wise with your time.

Profound life changes happen. Whether we feel ready for them or not, the Universe has a lovely way of giving us what we are ready for. Transformation is most often painful; physically, mentally, and emotionally. The key to less traumatic transitions lie in the state of our emotional well being. If a body is rigid during an accident it tends to sustain more injury. Loose and flexible bodies absorb the impact with less upheaval. Embrace your flexible body.

Having foresight is a superpower. Worry and anxiety rob us of the present moment, clouding the very future we attempt to create. Although contradictory, living in the here and now strengthens our ability to see ahead clearly. What we find is that looking forward is the same as looking backward; both directions take us away from enjoying what's right in front of us.

Hold yourself as a new mother would her baby. Listen to your breath and listen to the beating of your heart. Before you slip away to sleep, ponder your future, and give gratitude for your heart no matter what your state. Count your fingers and count your toes. Love yourself as a new mother loves her newborn.

Face a mirror. Spend a few moments with the face you were blessed with. Follow the lines of your brows to your nose, look into your eyes, notice the color on your cheeks and lips. Find favor in each intricate line, freckles, and lash. Worldly beauty is a blip on the timeline. Waste no more of who you are feeling dissatisfaction. You are beautiful, inside and out.

Please don't hide who you are. Your beauty lies in the complexities you embody, not the mask of perfection you wear. Compliment your least favorite feature today, show it love and honor it with a warm touch. Love for self starts with you.

The ability to laugh is a skill most coveted. It has been found that those that can laugh the hardest are souls that have experienced the most hardship. When it seems as if life is unbearable, pause, and bring your experiences into perspective. With effort, you can change the lens through which you view life, and find levity with the Cosmic Giggle.

For a moment, I embody the essence of a tree. As the roots reach down to provide the foundation -feet - the unwavering trunk, it represents my core. I will always remember that I am tall in strength, resiliency, and life-giving energy.

As you align more with your inner strength and desires, remember connecting with your dreams can be a missing piece to your puzzle. Throughout the day, say out loud "tonight, I will remember my dreams." Before you close tour eyes to sleep ask for assistance from the Universe to pull meaning from your sleep state.

Waking up to the reality of things can feel like a dissolution of everything I thought was true. As I jump forward into the unknown, Irely on our inner guidance, synchronicity, and divine intervention. I trust my process while you keep yourself from drifting back to sleep.

You are seamlessly walking your path now, believe that you will rise to the occasion each time it calls out. Hands of opportunity are reaching out for you, hold tight to them as you reach for the next steps to take.

Your dream career, life purpose and calling is building. Can you feel your awareness around it? Keep your spirits up as you enjoy the ride-- always keep the visualization by your side.

In this day and age, there are many barriers to human connection. Today I do not feel alone, and others are available for me in the ways that I need. I have created a community that shows up for one other you will attract all that you desire.

I enjoy laughter and I avidly seek it out. The moments I set aside to exercise my "laugh muscle" not only change my view of the world, and add days and years to my life, but laughs are infectious and spread quickly.

I offer the world healing when I identify how to bring healing to my inner world. The pressure is removed when I take time to remember that life is a continued practice of doing my best.

I take notice of all my curiosities in the world. The way my body reacts to stimuli in my life, the cycles of the planets and my connection to my ancestors. I enjoy what my imagination brings to my awareness and I enjoy learning new things.

My pulse in life beats together with the natural rhythm of nature. The Moons light always guides me through the darkness and when I wake, the Sun brings promise of a new day. I connect to this rhythm daily by feeling the subtle beat of my heart.

My relationships are blossoming, when I bring my whole self to the table, I am met with wholeness in return. I make it a point to say something kind and uplifting to someone I love today.

I give myself permission to change my mind. This simple idea relieves me from the pressure of living under old burdens and releases me from expired and no longer useful ideas.

My connection to nature is being restored. I will do my best to make sure I participate in walking through the trees barefoot, I will eat enlivened foods in abundance, and look up at the stars if out by a fire. I will be diligent and nurture my connection to nature.

I am stable and consistent as I build a solid foundation for myself and the people I hold dear. When I am able to gain proper footing, I receive the energy and guidance of the universe in everything I do.

I am composed of celestial magic. Each part of my body is a reflection of the Universe above. I have the power to effect change- both large and small because I radiate divine energy through my earthly body. I believe that you embody pure energy, here on the physical plane.

My life is full of meaning and being here on this planet is of no accident. When I was born, I was created with the divine spark of the cosmos and I contribute my life experience to the collective consciousness.

Truth is realative, there is individual truth and there is collective truth. What feels true for me wont always feel true for the next person. I will consider beliefs outside my framework to embrace diversity and new points of view.

I recognize my ability to shift my perspective as I gain new outlooks while living my unique life expression. I follow my intuitions, not my fears.

Living in this body is a challenge, but is extremely rewarding. When I feel discouraged, I will remember to hold tight to the feelings of gratitude and acceptance of my situation. The energy in my body keeps me seeking and motivated to continue on my path. I know to remember- one foot in front of the next.

I enjoy the company of the people I surround myself with and I love to share the frequency and vibration of good times with them. I know all I need to do is ask or reach out to my support group if I am in need of anything. I will be a vessel to hold others up, make space for them and offer guidance where needed.

I seek a relationship with myself in the same ways I look to seek relationship with others. I am my own soulmate. I establish open and true connection with my inner world and allow vulnerability to come into my life.

Today I am finding time to stare at the sky. I will notice the cool breeze on my skin, the heat of the Sun and the coolness of my drink as it splashes down my throat. I deserve the gift of enjoyment and the feeling of taking my time and enjoying the small things in life.

The next time I find myself in a moment of pure joy, I will pause and listen to the beating of my own heart. I will ask myself if I enjoy the way my life looks in its current state. I will look to feel wholeness in my decisions and actions. I recognize my feelings are a part of my divine connection to the universe and I know I am on the right path.

Printed in the USA
CPSIA information can be obtained
at www.ICGtesting.com
LVHW012215181223
766859LV00012B/670